THE
Company
WE
KEEP

New York Times bestselling author

ALEXANDRA ELLE

THE
Company
WE
KEEP

Friendship, Connection and Redefining What It Means to Grow Together

GALLERY BOOKS UK

London · New York · Amsterdam/Antwerp · Sydney/Melbourne · Toronto · New Delhi

First published in the United States by Tarcher, an imprint of
Penguin Random House, LLC, 2026

First published in Great Britain by Gallery Books, an imprint of
Simon & Schuster UK Ltd, 2026

Copyright © Alexandra Elle, 2026

The right of Alexandra Elle to be identified as the author of this work has been
asserted in accordance with the Copyright, Designs and Patents Act, 1988.

1 3 5 7 9 10 8 6 4 2

Simon & Schuster UK Ltd, 1st Floor,
222 Gray's Inn Road, London WC1X 8HB

www.simonandschuster.co.uk
www.simonandschuster.com.au
www.simonandschuster.co.in

Simon & Schuster Australia, Sydney
Simon & Schuster India, New Delhi

The authorised representative in the EEA is Simon & Schuster Netherlands BV,
Herculesplein 96, 3584 AA Utrecht, Netherlands. info@simonandschuster.nl

The author and publishers have made all reasonable efforts to contact copyright-
holders for permission, and apologise for any omissions or errors in the form of
credits given. Corrections may be made to future printings.

A CIP catalogue record for this book is available from the British Library

Hardback ISBN: 978-1-3985-5584-6
eBook ISBN: 978-1-3985-5586-0

Interior design by Angie Boutin

Printed and Bound in the UK using 100% Renewable Electricity
at CPI Group (UK) Ltd

For those learning to honor the seasons of their relationships—the ones who are choosing clarity without resentment, closeness without self-abandonment, and truth without fear. May this book be a companion as you gather with care, release with love, and remain open to the joy of being deeply known.

CONTENTS

PART TWO

THE
Company
WE
KEEP

INTRODUCTION

I N THESE PAGES, I'LL BE SHARING STORIES AND TOOLS TO help you look at yourself, and to take inventory of what and who is not working so that you can build and deepen the connections around you. Adult friendships are a beautiful gift—nurturing, layered, and sometimes complicated. We don't talk enough about how they shift and stretch with the seasons of our lives, yet that's just part of their rhythm. We all want to feel seen, safe, and supported in this life. We all deserve that. This book will help you zoom in and identify how to better show up, create clarity, and find peace in and out of your relationships. Over the years, I've learned that to reap the rewards of our soul work, we have to surround ourselves with people who support our evolution. Being on the same page with the ones we love is a gift, but it can be a task that isn't always comfortable. There will be moments in this book that will ask you to pause, reflect, and be radically honest about where you are in your life and relationships. Looking at what *is* instead of what we want things to be, will open the door for deeper truth and connection. If we continue to give our time to the people who want to keep us small, resent our successes, or judge our dreams, we can't truly experience the benefits of our inner work. If we keep pouring our energy into people who hold us back, dislike our evolution, or discredit our ambitions, we'll struggle to truly feel the power of genuine community and camaraderie. This journey is about making room for those who uplift us, looking at ourselves and how we need to adjust, and building reciprocal relationships that support growth and healing.

In 2022, I decided it was time to be more intentional and honest about my friendships and how I showed up in them. It started unexpectedly. I thought I was simply trying to be clearer about what I wanted, needed, and expected in my relationships and vice versa. But as that journey to clarity and honesty unfolded, it became apparent that what I was really doing was asking: Are my friendships—both old and new—still sustainable? And am I showing up fully and authentically for the people I care about?

The people around us shape us. They can influence so much in our lives, from how we speak and think, to how we deal with conflict. And depending on who we're with, certain things shift. Some friends make us feel like we're returning home to ourselves, welcoming every facet of who we are without judgment, while others leave us feeling slightly out of place and maybe even unsure. I realized that standing in my authenticity required me to stay close to people who saw me fully, welcomed me wholly, and had the capacity to walk with me even through rocky terrain.

Thankfully, I am fortunate to have some wonderful friends willing to work with me to strengthen our ties. Deepening those bonds has been a gift. But, just as painfully, I had to face the truth that some relationships I had carried for years no longer reflected where I was or where I was headed. That wasn't an easy pill to swallow, but evolution rarely is.

What becomes clearer to me as I embark on this path of alignment in my relationships is that I desire to have people in my life who encourage and support me through the ups and downs like I do them. One-sided relationships are no longer an option for me. They've never been supportive or fruitful. I deeply value having a community of like-minded individuals who share similar intentions and values. As I've matured, I've seen firsthand that I don't need a lot of people in my life to feel cared for or deeply loved. My circle is small, but my confidants provide a big safe space for vulnerability, togetherness, and unfolding. There is no one-size-fits-all approach to friendship circles: I thrive with a small network, but others bloom with a large group of friends spread across the globe. I can't tell you how many friends to have, but I can tell you that you deserve people in your life who help you get through the mud and stand in your joy. This is priceless. Not only that, it is possible. This is why I believe so deeply that the company we keep matters in a major way. The time, attention, and care that we invest in one another so generously is fuel for our relationships.

Something I've longed for since childhood were people who made me feel safe and held, emotionally, physically, and mentally. It's human to want connection with others that feels comforting and secure. I think everyone does to some extent. I spent a lot of my young adult life not knowing how or where to find my people. Having folks in our lives who make us feel witnessed, cherished, and celebrated for who we truly are is a gift. A good support system is sacred. Being held through the toughest of times with steady love and encouragement is a reminder that we all need to be poured into. There's a different type of emotional freedom that comes from honest and clear relationships that is unmatched. Knowing that you can show up as your full, authentic self without fear of judgment or rejection is liberating. This book is about discovering, nurturing, and thriving with the people we're choosing to do life with. It's about honesty, acceptance, and adjusting along the way. I want you to get excited about building these intentional connections because the reward is a life enriched with genuine support, clarity, and compassion, along with mutual growth. Together, we'll explore how to create powerful and transformative relationships that will enhance your life and empower you to be more mindful, clear, and honest.

I hope that you see yourself in my personal stories, vows to stay myself, and the many lessons learned. You'll see that at times I've gotten it right, and other times I've gotten it dead wrong. I've experienced the turmoil that comes with losing relationships, and the gratitude that settles in after the grief subsides. I've welcomed joyful relationships after loss, and I've discovered what it means to be a good friend and fit for others. Every instance has planted a deeper seed of self-awareness and reflection. With time and age, I've learned that we must be who we seek in the world. We are not alone in finding our people. A turning point in all of this was making a list of vows I promised myself I wouldn't stray from. My healing journey has taught me that if I want others to honor me, I must first honor myself and keep the promises I make to my own heart. I had to let go of expecting people to hold me in the same light I held them, especially when I wasn't cradling myself with that same care and reverence.

I knew I was ready to deepen my relationship with myself and others when I vowed to:

- Honor my boundaries as a form of self-respect, and trust that those who truly see me will respect them, too.

- Choose reciprocity over resentment, prioritizing relationships rooted in honest communication, care, and intention.

- Speak with honesty, even when it feels uncomfortable, knowing that truth builds stronger connections.

- Release relationships that no longer align with who I am becoming, without guilt or shame, but with gratitude for the lessons they brought.

- Welcome the friendships that feel like home, allowing me to lean into the joy of being seen and valued fully.

- Remain open to change, understanding that growth sometimes requires shifting, repair, or letting go.

- Hold myself accountable for how I show up in relationships, practicing clarity, care, and intention in every interaction.

- Trust that there are people who will meet me in the love and effort I give and that I do not need to shrink myself to keep anyone close.

I would encourage everyone reading this book to make your own vow list. Getting clear about what you are willing to deal with and what you're not—on all fronts, not just friendships—will create a road map for your journey to clarity and connection. I know this path can be quite rocky, but please trust that there are folks out there looking for you, too. All of us are trying to figure out how to move in love and create healthy, intentional relationships—and with that comes the willingness to do the work. Understanding ourselves and others is filled with ebbs and flows. We know this and see it on a daily basis. Relationships of every kind are rarely straightforward or linear, but a deep joy can emerge when cultivating a community that nourishes rather than depletes. Looking closely at our friendships and the vows we make to ourselves makes more room for us to name what is aligned and what is not. Friendship is a practice. Connection requires accountability, compassion, and self-awareness. Collectively, moving intentionally in our relationships summons both courage and care. It's a way of saying: *I'm choosing to move with clarity and openness with myself and those ready to walk alongside me.*

Holding up a mirror to the relationship we have with ourselves is a key part of that process. Many folks are moving through the world unwilling to do their soul work or not ready to embark on their healing. This is unfortunate and can ultimately lead to chaotic relationships crumbling in confusion, and that is not the goal. The goal is to create a healthy inner world so that we can foster healthy relationships with others. This will require us to show up for ourselves and be realistic about what and who we are dealing with. It's an invitation to look at our flaws and theirs without judgment while tapping into what accountability, trust, and self-awareness mean for us in the season we're in. I used to be one of the people who refused to address how I was showing up, good or bad. That took a lot of unlearning, intentional shifting, and tough sessions with my therapist to unpack and redirect. It's hard enough to trust ourselves with our own hearts, let alone the hearts of others. But as we embark on this journey of healthy connection and clear communication, self-trust is an absolute must.

As you read this book, I hope you learn to surrender to the truth that you're capable of being in nourishing and nurturing relationships. You are worthy of being a part of others' core group, even if you're feeling out of place or lonely right now. This journey is not just about finding your people—it's also about letting your people find you. As we evolve and learn to be more present in our relationships, we'll start to lean deeper into the importance of creating space for our community to take shape. The intention is to be open to giving as much as we receive, listening as much as we speak, and supporting as much as we seek support. Remember, this work has no arrival point, just constant evolution. It's about embracing the ongoing process of growth and change, and understanding that each step forward is a valuable part of our journey.

In gratitude,

Alex Elle

A NOTE BEFORE YOU BEGIN

PART ONE IS PART MEMOIR, PART MIRROR—MY STORY, my learnings, and a gentle nudge for you to re-examine the company you keep.

Part Two is an offering of practice—rooted in story-telling, guided reflection, and tools to help you navigate what comes next.

May peace and clarity meet you where you are on this journey.

PART
ONE

COMMUNICATION AND CARE

*W*HILE I WAS MAKING MYSELF A CUP OF COFFEE, THE chime of my iPhone dinged with a message from one of my closest friends, B. We normally spoke multiple times a week, if not multiple times a day. We'd gotten into a rhythm of checking in, even if just to give each other a heads-up that we'd be busy and our regular scheduled communication would be interrupted by adulting, work, and life with little room for balance. But not this week. She had been quiet for a few days, which I hadn't experienced before. The energy was off, but I couldn't put my finger on why. In my heart, I felt something was going on with her, and I wanted to make sure she was okay. I made a mental note to call her at some point to see how she was doing. The friendship was fairly new, and since we were still learning each other, I didn't want to push or pry if she was having a tough time. Something I valued about our bond, even though the connection was young, was that we knew, without question, that we were safe with each other. Safe to say how and what we were feeling— safe to be honest, unjudged, and fully ourselves, even if things weren't feeling great internally. From the beginning, our connection felt uncomplicated and easeful, regardless of the stuff life threw our way. I was confident she would reach out when she was ready. And she did, a few minutes after I reminded myself to check on her.

> B: Hey girl, I just wanted to let you know that this weekend has been hard for me, so if I've been quiet or giving different energy the past couple of days, that's why. My partner and I had our first misunderstanding. Things will be okay, but I am sad and trying to process what happened. Right now, I'm feeling extra tender.

When I read her message, I felt a mix of concern and gratitude. Concern for what she was going through, and gratitude for the trust she placed in me by sharing her vulnerability. Vulnerability builds emotional safety and

I'd literally been praying for that type of communication in friendship. Her trust in me to hold what she was going through, felt like an honor and a stepping stone in our growing friendship. It's amazing that something as simple as being clear about how we're feeling can foster such depth and reverence. Having people who value us as we value them creates a lightness in our life. Placing my fresh cup of coffee on the counter, I responded immediately, letting her know I was there for her, ready to listen whenever needed.

ME: Thank you for sharing. Please let me know if you want to talk about it. I'm here for you.

As I hit SEND, I reflected on emotional safety and how hard I've worked to get to a place in my relationships to cultivate it. It felt good to read that message from B. It showed that we were truly on the same page when it came to being honest, clear, and present. It would've been easier for her to stay in a bubble, not share what she was going through, and come back around when she was ready. Our friendship was new, but it felt kindred and aligned. Our values, communication style, and consideration for the people in our lives felt foundational and important. I've had friendships dissolve at the first sign of discomfort. While I understand that when life happens, people can retreat, the lack of communication, begging to know what's wrong, and sometimes outright ghosting wasn't something I was willing to tolerate in my relationships anymore. The care that B showed our friendship by leaning into vulnerability was a green flag for me. It made me feel extremely grateful for how far we'd both come in our healing, growth, and emotional maturity. There's nothing better than having positive actions match the words people say to us.

Over the years, I've come to understand that having the capacity to create a safe space for the ones we love isn't just about being there during the good times, but also about creating a space where it's truly okay to be not alright—to have the confidence to say, *I'm quiet because . . .* versus shutting down and closing people out from your life. Emotional safety means knowing you can authentically express your feelings without fear of judgment or rejection. Creating this type of care in our connections with others is the footing that allows friendships to weather storms and grow stronger through challenges.

Like most new friendships, the early stages are like navigating uncharted waters. B and I were learning each other's likes, dislikes, and boundaries. But from the start, there was a mutual understanding that we could be honest and open—this didn't happen by accident. We both consciously chose to prioritize true connection with vulnerability, reciprocity, and care. Nurturing our relationships is a delicate dance of discovery that requires intention and trust. Every conversation reveals a new layer of personality, a new facet of character, and a better understanding about how to connect.

I thought back to the first time B and I met. She'd reached out to me and generously offered to be the photographer for my Washington, DC, book tour stop at the Howard Theatre, as a gift. I wasn't familiar with her work and did some research—only to find out she was one of the best photographers in the city, whose work had been featured everywhere. I was beyond honored and grateful. We didn't talk much that night but her kind energy spoke to me. I knew that I wanted to get a chance to sit down and get to know her. As a thank you, I invited her out for tea and a bite to eat at a local coffee shop. There was an immediate connection of sisterhood, a sense of ease that felt comforting, clear, and aligned. From our first sit-down at Tatte Café, the soul work we both had done was very evident, giving us the space to be available for each other without hesitation. There was very little small talk. We dove right into sharing our lives, healing, fears, joys, and everything else. Meeting at Tatte became a thing we did regularly after that. Our bond solidified after each coffee date, photo walk, and phone call with these moments of vulnerability.

A year or so had passed since then, and now we were facing our first moment of crisis in one of our lives in real time. A couple of days after she texted me about her challenging weekend, we hopped on the phone. B's voice was soft but steady when we spoke. She recounted the misunderstanding with her partner, and her words were filled with compassion, tenderness, and trust in her relationship and herself. I listened, offering support and reassurance without trying to fix anything. Sometimes, all we need is someone to hear, acknowledge, and remind us that we're not alone. As our conversation wound down, I felt a renewed appreciation for the emotional safety we developed. We'd come so far since that first meeting in 2022. It was a reminder that genuine friendship is not always measured by the time we've known someone but by the depth of our connection and willingness to trust and be trusted. What this experience with B showed me, is that being there for each other and creating a space to be our authentic self is an act of emotional nourishment even in our hushed and tender moments.

In the following days, we continued to check in with each other. The lightness and cadence we had returned with ease. Through this, I learned that emotional safety is not just a cornerstone of friendship but a gift we give to each other. It's a reminder that the company we keep matters and that we deserve to be in relationships with people who choose us, see us, and lovingly accept us. An unspoken comfort comes from knowing we are seen, heard, and loved exactly as we are.

Creating healthy dynamics in our relationships requires effort and intention. If we are not present, mindful of how we show up, or clear with our communication, we risk being misaligned and disconnected.

Over the years, I've realized that I've often been a friend to others, but they haven't always been a friend to me. Initially, this felt painful, leading to feelings of rejection and disappointment, paired with thoughts of why can't this person show up fully with me, like I do with them? The answer to that is a simple but hard truth—we are not the same. Everyone is different. That's not always good or bad—it's just different. I no longer view someone else's inability or unwillingness to show up as a negative in my life. Taking things personally that are not about us isn't beneficial. Instead, I've learned one of the greatest lessons: You can't force alignment or communication. Sometimes, the connections we believe we have are simply misaligned. This misalignment can look like unmet expectations, mismatched values, or differing levels of emotional investment. It can manifest as feeling misunderstood, unsupported, or drained after interactions, even without obvious conflict. We may find ourselves giving more than we receive, feeling unheard, or realizing that the connection no longer supports our growth. While these relationships may have served us at one point, holding on to them out of comfort can lead to resentment, unhealthy communication, and eventually distance. What you consider a meaningful and aligned connection might not resonate in the same way for someone else, and that's okay. Recognizing this allows us to make space for healthier relationships that nurture both parties meaningfully. What may have once felt like a bond of mutual understanding may not stay that way. While it's natural for relationships to change, recognizing the misalignment is a sign that we need to reevaluate some things.

In this season of my life, I'm choosing people who choose me, prioritizing those who value our connection, and making space for nourishing reciprocal relationships. I feel blessed to have a small group of friends who actively listen, validate feelings, and show unwavering empathy. They are my winning circle, the ones—like B—that I can count on and trust with my full self, and vice versa. Having the energy and space to be physically and emotionally available deepens our connection to those we say we love. Building a trust that neither time nor distance can diminish is sacred. Being able to say to the people in our lives, *My energy is off right now because I am going through something that has nothing to do with you . . .* without fear of rejection is unmatched. This intentional shift reflects a deeper understanding of what it means to truly connect with others and the importance of being selective about the relationships we nurture.

The more I heal, the more I strive to create and nurture emotional safety and clarity in my relationships. We find true connection and lasting bonds in these safe spaces.

Having clear, honest conversations about our needs and expectations has been incredibly helpful in forming my circle of aligned relationships. If I had experienced this situation with B in my early twenties, I would have taken her quietness personally and assumed she didn't want to be friends. Drastic, I know, but without the right tools, we often jump to conclusions.

It wasn't until my thirties that I began to practice using my words and being vulnerable about my feelings within my platonic relationships. Early in B's and my friendship, I opened up to her about my anxieties regarding making new friends. She was my first new connection in a long time. I admitted how frightening it was for me to connect with people. I had spent many years in various relationships, walking on eggshells, constantly fearing I might say or do something to disrupt the fragile bonds. Yet I also shared my desire for friendships with women who valued healthy communication, consistency, and authentic connection. This conversation marked a turning point. She heard me loud and clear. Having her validate that with her own stories and experiences was a relief. And it allowed us to build a deeper, more meaningful relationship grounded in clarity and mutual understanding.

It felt good to know that other women were out there looking for the same thing and could show up in the ways I was committed to.

The discomfort was, and sometimes can still be, *very* real, but these conversations are essential. They involve a level of openness that can stretch us and our relationships

for the better—they can deepen our friendship foundations and create more authentic connections. We set the
stage for relationships built on mutual respect and understanding by discussing our capacity to meet each other's
expectations. Talking openly, honestly, and compassionately with people who make us feel seen, safe, and supported is a game-changer. I want friends who will say, *I'm
quiet because* . . . versus vanishing and expecting things to
be all fine and good when they resurface. I want people in
my life who can say, *That hurt my feelings,* or *I need some
space* . . . versus running away at the first sign of conflict.

Often, I find that many of us weren't taught to use our
words and communicate our feelings in healthy ways. In
adulthood, I take pride in doing my best to deepen this
practice. Having B reach out and share what she was going
through validated that it is possible to be in reciprocal and
like-minded connections and cultivate genuinely enriching
relationships.

That experience with her fundamentally altered my
perspective, shifting my focus from the number of friends
I have to the quality of relationships I chose to nurture. I
had been caught in a spiral of self-doubt, convinced that
my lack of "a lot of friends" was the reason why my interactions felt hollow, misaligned, and unsupportive. It seemed
logical that more friends would lead to more fulfilling connections. However, through my experience with B and
other friends who were on a healing path similar to mine,

I came to a pivotal realization: The number of friends is insignificant compared to the quality and depth of those relationships. Meeting you in your healing will be challenging if folks aren't doing their soul work. Trying to force connections, clarity, and communication is not friendship rooted in ease. It's one entangled in struggle and chaos, which no one wants.

True connection arises from the inner work individuals have done. It is important to find friends who have navigated their journeys of healing and growth. Not everyone is equipped to meet us at our current stage of life, especially when our paths split. Our journeys may intersect at various points, but expecting others to change or grow at our pace is often unrealistic and unfair—to them and to ourselves. Waiting for others to reach a point of understanding and healing can be a fruitless endeavor, especially when they are still discovering themselves.

Staying close to people who were walking a path similar to mine enriched my life and deepened my meaning of friendship and trust. How B and I communicate has taught me the importance of aligning with people who are like-minded. Because we value ourselves and each other, we are able to be present and in tune in meaningful and honest ways. This adjustment, albeit not an easy one, made such a difference in my life. It reminded me that there are people who will walk beside me, even when our inner worlds tremble. True grounding comes from being surrounded by those committed to their own inner work, who meet us in our authenticity. Over time, I realized I had been leading with a scarcity mindset, searching for connections in the wrong places. I often overlooked those already capable of offering true reciprocity. Finding community and care is difficult when we're chasing attention from people who can't meet us where we need to be met.

I went from feeling I lacked friends to noticing those already walking beside me. This shift deepened my relationships, revealing the richness already present. Letting go of the scarcity mindset I once clung to opened my heart to the abundance and support that was always there.

Sometimes there are moments when we feel like we don't have enough—enough friends, enough support, enough closeness—only to realize there are people ready for us to welcome them. This shift in perspective deepened my relationships, revealing the richness that was waiting for me to notice it. Before I met B, I was inching closer and closer to Team No New Friends category. I'd experienced so much frustration and letdown with others, I thought throwing in the towel and shutting off from folks was my only option. But we all know that shutting down and hardening our heart doesn't lead us closer to what we want, but instead pushes us further away from the lives we desire and deserve. Letting go of that fear-based mindset, and not allowing the hurt of my past to dictate the now or my future, shifted a lot of things for the better. Opening my heart to B showed me that the abundance and support that I was looking for were absolutely within my reach.

When the energy we invest in our relationships is reciprocated, that mutual investment means both parties feel valued and appreciated, which is crucial for connection and cultivating respect and emotional safety. It took me a long time, but by prioritizing reciprocity and intentionality, I have created a support system that fosters emotional well-being and encourages personal growth. Unwavering trust is evident when someone can say how they feel in a compassionate, caring, and considerate way without backlash. Many of us were not taught how to be in relationships like this—which is why, more often than not, our circles of people are rough around the edges instead of seamless and smooth.

I've come to realize that I desire to deepen the connections I have that enhance my overall quality of life—the ones that provide a safe space for emotional expression, personal development, and mutual support. I spent so long in misaligned relationships that felt draining and emotionally chaotic. Going back there isn't an option for me, and I no longer feel bad for standing ten toes down on that choice. I now have a circle of friends who text me after my child's first day of school to ask how it went, who answer my question *"How are you?"* honestly, and who listen to me even when I am complaining—and who can tell me when it's time to stop.

Finding and maintaining these deeper, more meaningful relationships is transformative in a world where superficial connections are often the norm, ghosting is the go-to, and fleeing at the first sign of friction is encouraged. People are quick to say something is a boundary when it's actually a barrier of fear hindering their ability to be in the healthy relationships they say they want. If I've learned anything on this relationship road it's that we won't get the tools we need to function in healthy ways without practice or openness. I think it's important to stay close to people who want to stay close to us. Those relationships reinforce our commitment to showing up authentically, communicating honestly and kindly, and prioritizing resolution, reciprocity, and repair.

The connections we choose to nurture will elevate us or keep us stuck. It is up to us to decide what is most important when it comes to the company we keep and the connections we nurture.

B's vulnerability reminded me that I am worthy and capable of being in friendships that honor the importance of mutual effort and shared values. I am less focused on the relationships that haven't evolved or lasted and more attentive to the ones that truly align with my values and who are willing to invest in our connection. Creating a supportive, enriching, and genuinely fulfilling community is possible. It is attainable to have ease, flow, commitment, and joy in every facet of our lives—alone and in community with others. Even if your circle is small, it can be mighty and meaningful.

It was a striking realization that I deserve connections where both parties are equally invested and dedicated to peace. This understanding has shifted my focus away from harping on the relationships that haven't evolved or lasted and toward cherishing those that genuinely align with my values and life path.

I now prioritize connections built on a foundation of mutual respect and shared intentions. These are the relationships where effort is not one-sided but a harmonious dance of giving and receiving, fostering growth and understanding. Recognizing the importance of this creates a supportive, enriching, and genuinely fulfilling community. It is not just a possibility—it is a reality within our reach.

People who truly understand and support each other can create a sense of belonging and fulfillment that uplifts and nourishes.

Reflections

- Think about the people in your life today—do they inspire ease and provide a sense of comfort? Or do they bring you chaos and confusion? How do these individuals align with your values and aspirations, or not?

- Consider how your current relationships impact your life. Do these connections contribute to your well-being and joy? Or are they holding you back and keeping you stuck?

- How do you show up in your relationships? Which connections do you want to nurture more? Which ones do you want to work on minimizing?

- Take a moment to identify your values and aspirations. How do these shape the people you want to surround yourself with? Reflect on past experiences where you felt connected to individuals who aligned with your values and aspirations.

In this season of my life, I'm choosing people who choose me, prioritizing those who value our connection, and making space for nourishing reciprocal relationships.

TWO

CREATING SPACE FOR HONESTY

OVER THE YEARS, I'VE GROWN TO VALUE OPENNESS, honesty, and healthy communication. It wasn't always like that. In fact, I was bad at it for most of my life. I wanted to develop close connections but lacked the tools and awareness to know how to do that. When you spend most of your life, like I did, not knowing how to use your words, or being too scared to use them for fear of being shunned, beaten, or punished, dysfunction and unhealthy silence become the norm. I wasn't taught how to speak up or encouraged to advocate for myself. I could either go along to get along or sit down and shut up. Both encouraged me to swallow my tongue and shrink myself into oblivion. The older I get, the more I understand that I and the people I have in my life deserve clarity, consideration, and commitment to making an effort to show up. Sometimes, it feels safer to shut down, perform, or pretend—rather than speak our truth. The problem with shutting down is that our relationships start to quietly wither. I remember when masking my true self was my go-to. Offering only what I thought others wanted. It was second nature for me to supply a smile when deep down I was filled with discomfort—and when things became too overwhelming, it was easy for me to retreat and get quiet. However, the more I hid, the more I found myself adrift, disconnected, and dishonest. I was constantly out of alignment and scared to get on the right track. It wasn't until I embraced myself fully and started respecting where I was, without the need to perform, that I began to feel truly seen. In allowing my vulnerability to surface, I felt less fearful about external judgment and could start welcoming those who could meet me as I was. And in that honesty, my relationships bloomed, rich with the depth I had been searching for all along.

When we are trapped in a cycle of silence, we have convinced ourselves that staying quiet protects us from making mistakes or saying the wrong thing, but it doesn't. These self-imposed gag orders seem like a shield, a way to avoid conflict, rejection, and judgment. But in reality, it was a barrier that kept me from expressing my true feelings, needs, and thoughts. It created walls that others could not permeate, and to be frank, it was mean. My default response to tension or discomfort was to retreat, hoping things would magically improve without confrontation. However, sweeping issues under the rug doesn't make them disappear; it only creates a lumpy, unstable surface on which to build our lives. The walls I put up looked like unanswered texts, not being vulnerable, holding things in that bothered me then exploding about it later, or just cutting people off altogether, none of which created the closeness I said I wanted, which made people feel insecure in their friendship with me. I lacked graciousness and avoided conflict out of immaturity and fear. It took many years to learn and trust that healthy confrontation is good. It can be a beautiful catalyst for radical honesty, loving-kindness, and respect.

My avoidance turned into a habit, one that bred emotional junk, resentment, and dysfunction. I lacked clarity and curiosity about how my actions would make someone else feel. I made excuses for not showing up fairly with sentiments like, *I don't owe anyone anything, and these are my boundaries,* when, in reality, I was scared to tell the truth. I feared that speaking up might turn something small into something major, but I failed to see or acknowledge that my silence was inflicting the greatest harm. When we are in intimate relationships with people and suddenly, without explanation, ghost them and cease to show up, authentic connections cannot be built. Instead, walls are erected where bridges and open lines of dialogue are needed. My relationships suffered because I couldn't bring myself to voice my truths, and this erosion of communication undermined trust and intimacy.

I like to think of unspoken words as stones we collect, tucking them away in every corner of our being, hoping they won't eventually weigh us down—but they will. Each unexpressed emotion, each withheld truth, becomes a weight we silently bear. At first, we believe we can manage the load, but over time, those stones grow heavier, pressing down on us until we're on the verge of collapse. Silence, once our refuge, slowly morphs into a burden, and the weight of what remains unsaid begins to tear at the seams of our lives.

What we carry in silence eventually finds a voice, but not in gentle whispers—it erupts in the form of frustration, resentment, or heartache. Our unsaid words, once manageable, now scream from within, leaving us exhausted, disconnected, and distanced from the people we care about. One of my greatest lessons has been the realization that holding it all in chips away at the foundations of our soul and our relationships, and creates a divide between us and genuine connection.

I thought silence protected me for years and was a safe

place to retreat. But I came to realize it was really a hushed destroyer, deteriorating trust and preventing closeness. The truth is, when we use silence as a shield or a weapon, we build walls that keep us from true closeness. To build meaningful relationships, we first have to confront the stones we've been hoarding, acknowledge their weight, and make the choice to set them down. Only then can we make space for vulnerability, truth, and the kind of connection rooted in something real.

Looking back, I see that my silence was a loud cry for connection, albeit an unhealthy one. When we leave things unsaid in hopes that they go unnoticed and finally return to normal, we leave a trail of fractured relationships and missed opportunities for deeper understanding. To have healthy and restorative connections, we need to be willing to address the hard thing head-on. If I wanted my relationships to be rooted in clarity and honesty, it was up to me to break harmful habits and unhealthy patterns in big and small ways. There was a lot for me to unlearn and face—and it took time and consistent practice. I used to avoid difficult conversations, afraid that speaking my truth would lead to conflict or rejection. I would agree to things I didn't want in order to keep the peace, or stay silent when I was hurt, believing that my feelings weren't important enough to voice. I also habitually overextended myself, saying yes to others' needs while neglecting my own, thinking that my worth was tied to how much I could give.

One day, it struck me how often I had been building relationships on shaky foundations by not being honest. Time and time again, I agreed to plans I didn't want to do to avoid letting someone down. In those moments, I wasn't just bending—I was betraying myself and lying to someone else, who I know would much rather I be straightforward. That quiet discomfort became a teacher, showing me how much communication and transparency matter—not just for the health of the relationship but for the harmony within my own heart. So I started small. I began saying no when I meant it, even if it felt uncomfortable. I practiced expressing my feelings, even when I feared how they might be received. I stopped pretending to be okay when I wasn't. Though difficult, these changes were liberating and deepened my connections. It wasn't an effortless task, but each step toward authenticity brought me closer to the kinds of relationships I had always wanted—ones built on truth and mutual respect.

When silence and pretense become your default, dysfunction is inevitable. Misunderstandings fester, resentment builds, and trust gets tarnished. Without honest communication, we can't resolve conflict, clear up misconceptions, or express our true selves. And we cannot make space to hold the feelings and hearts of others. Instead, we wear masks, bite our tongue, and stifle our authenticity. This doesn't just cause harm to us, it ends up hurting others. Sooner than later, I learned that this is unsustainable and unkind. Unlearning this required me to take a hard look at myself, stop making excuses and dressing my silence as a boundary, and start being real and honest about the time and space I had to share with others.

A few years ago, a woman I had been close friends with in the past reached out to me and wanted to reconnect. We'd drifted apart, not because anything adverse had happened but because our lives and capacities had changed. We each had more kids, we lived in different states, and the seasons that we were in as women, mothers, and wives were not aligned. The disconnect did not feel bad. It just felt different. Both of us tried our best to stay in touch, but eventually communication slowed and then stopped.

The day I heard from her, I was happy. Eager to get back to her, I smiled and immediately replied to her voice memo. However, after a short text exchange, reality kicked in. I knew I had no space to reconnect—even though I thought I should. At one point, this woman had been a good friend. I felt obligated to figure out how to fit her back into my life. So I toiled with how I could do that intentionally. Earlier that year, I vowed that I wanted to avoid investing in surface-level relationships. This shift was inspired by a period of reflection on the friendships I had maintained over the years and the ones that had faded away. I saw a pattern of giving more than I received or investing in relationships that didn't align with my values or needs. Like everyone else, my life was busy—but I wasn't willing to let that be an excuse for settling for connections that lacked depth. I wanted friendships rooted in honesty, where we could be real with one another, even if that realness meant some felt disappointed—but still loved, nonetheless. This vow marked a turning point that shaped how I approached friendship moving forward—seeking relationships that felt authentic, intentional, and deeply reciprocal.

I didn't think superficial friendships were fair to anyone, especially those looking for closeness and true community. And while she was eager to jump right back where we left off, it had been more than a year of little to no communication. She was ready to align our calendars so we could schedule a call or FaceTime, but I immediately felt overwhelmed by adding another thing to my plate. And I was wrestling with the fact that I didn't just *not* have the time—I didn't *want* to make the time. I was unwilling to put another thing on my calendar. I was unwilling to make the effort it took to press PLAY again on our paused friendship. Emotionally, I didn't have the will to add another connection back into the rotation of my life. And that felt mean and harsh. I liked her and valued what we had back then, but I couldn't just pick up where we'd left off. That felt impossible and like a heavier lift than I had the strength for. A part of me wanted to go silent because that would've been much easier than facing the facts—but I wasn't doing that anymore. In this moment of clarity, I realized something profound about relationships. Being in them and making time for them are choices we must make. It is essential to honor where we are in our lives and to recognize that it's okay to set boundaries, even with people we care about deeply. Relationships ebb and flow, and sometimes it's not about the worthiness of the other person but about our capacity. I realistically could not hold her with the care and attention she deserved. Forcing reconnection or friendship is more harmful to our bonds than telling the truth—even if it's a hard one. Community care sometimes means making tough decisions and telling the truth. Recognizing when we cannot give our best to a relationship is a generous act of honesty and kindness.

The guilt I felt about this weighed heavy on my heart. I started to feel awful about this reckoning. I so wanted to be like the women I've heard boasting on podcasts and social media about not talking to someone for months or years and resuming like no time had passed when they crossed paths again. I felt a little envious, even. Like, why can't that be me? But I'm not that girl. So much had changed, and I liked the ease and flow of things as they were. My life was filled to the brim with family stuff, work, and making an intentional effort to nurture my small circle of friends. I'd gotten into a groove. Instead of wallowing in shame and guilt, I chose to be honest with her.

With compassion and care, I told her I didn't have the time or space to connect. And after so much time had passed, I didn't want to rush our conversation, knowing that I was filled to the brim. This honesty, I hoped, would be a foundation for any future reconnection should our paths align again. She was understanding and grateful. Her reply was equally kind and honest. *I get it, completely—life has been so busy and I am just now coming back up for air. I miss you and look forward to reconnecting when time allows,* she texted back.

I've learned over the years that acknowledging the truth of what is, can maintain meaningful connections, even if they've taken on a new shape. Honesty is a nod to respecting each other's journeys. It honors that there's a time and place for everything and everyone. Every day, I learn to recognize the benefits of honoring the natural rhythms of relationships instead of going along to get along. And in doing so, we create a more intentional and fulfilling life that reflects our true selves and respects our emotional and mental boundaries.

The more I heal and work on myself, the more I realize that clarity in communication is a gift we give to ourselves and others. It fosters understanding, empathy, and connection in a way that silence could never. It's a gracious way to exercise our responsibility to those we are in a relationship with. When we are clear about our feelings, needs, and boundaries, we create fertile ground where authenticity and compassion can take root and flourish.

Sound communication begins with self-awareness. Tools like revisiting the vows you made for yourself, practicing self-check-ins, or even writing down your needs before a difficult conversation, can help you clarify what's actually true in that moment. For example, instead of saying, *"I'm fine,"* when you're not, try: *"I'm feeling overwhelmed and need a little time to process before we talk about this."* I know this feels easier said than done, letting people down isn't comfortable, but it gets easier with practice and cultivates deeper trust in the long run.

We succeed in setting boundaries and clarity in communication when we express our needs without guilt or apology, such as saying, *"I can't commit to that right now, but I appreciate you thinking of me,"* or *"I value our time together, but I need space to recharge after a busy week."* We stumble when we avoid confrontation out of fear, say yes out of obligation, or allow resentment to build because we haven't communicated our limits. For me, a sign of success is when a relationship feels lighter and more respectful after being honest and clear. On the other hand, a red flag I've started to pay more attention to is when boundaries are ignored or when vulnerability is met with dismissal or defensiveness. None of this is easy, but when done with openness and consideration, it fosters deeper trust and harmony for yourself and the people around you. Knowing that we are being cared for intentionally is a beautiful feeling. Honest communication will not always be easy or comfortable, but it can show that we value and respect people, their time, and their feelings.

Telling my old friend I didn't want to reconnect was hard; it required vulnerability and courage to be honest instead of forcing a friendship that was no longer a priority. It also required a sense of emotional safety to be able to be this honest. I knew I could be open with her without her hating, blaming, or shaming me. She is someone I care about, and vice versa, and meeting her where and how she was asking me to was not too much, but at that time, I was unable to. The weight of my own responsibilities and emotional struggles made it difficult to show up in the way she needed. While I understood her desires and intentions, my internal state was overwhelmed, leaving me incapable of offering the level of support and presence she deserved. In hindsight, I recognize that it wasn't about her requests being unreasonable, but about my limits at that moment and how I needed to first address what was happening within me before I could fully be there for her.

In the past, I would have gone along to get along or vanished, which doesn't serve my overall well-being or authentic connections. I honestly admitted that I didn't have the time or the space to connect. She shared that she, too, had been navigating her own challenges and appreciated the clarity I offered. It wasn't the conversation we once might have had, full of laughter and shared experiences, but it was a necessary moment of respect for each other's boundaries. By acknowledging where we were in our lives, we left the door open for a future where we could reconnect more deeply when we both had the emotional bandwidth to engage with the care our friendship deserved.

The reward of staying true to yourself and being truthful with the people we surround ourselves with deepens our connections and strengthens our integrity. Honesty is often daunting because it requires us to be vulnerable. We fear our true selves or reasoning for certain things will be rejected or misconceived. However, it is through truthfulness that we build faith in one another and emotional intimacy. Something I had to remember, especially when telling someone that I couldn't show up intentionally, was that honesty about the time and space we have doesn't mean being harsh or unkind. If anything, it can be a nurturing and courteous act, even though sometimes being true to yourself may look like letting someone else down. It means expressing our feelings without blaming others, stating our needs without demanding, and setting boundaries without shutting people out. One of the biggest barriers to honest communication is the fear of rejection. This fear is deeply rooted in our desire for acceptance and belonging. However, it's important to remember that true connection can only be built on authenticity. When we are honest, we make room for others to know and love us for who we truly are. This kind of acceptance is far more fulfilling than the superficial approval we might receive by pretending to be someone we're not.

Sure, I could've gone along to get along with my friend, but that wouldn't have served our connection in the long run. No one wants to feel like they fit uncomfortably into the lives of others. People want healthy, honest, and reciprocal relationships. When we commit to sincere, genuine, and thoughtful communication, we transform our relationships. We move from a place of misunderstanding and resentment to empathy and openness. This transformation doesn't happen overnight. It asks us to practice, be patient, and be willing to stand tall in authenticity and reality. We step toward deeper, more meaningful relationships whenever we show up honestly.

The older I get, the more I appreciate people who match my effort. There's nothing like connecting with folks who genuinely want you to feel heard, seen, and valued. Reciprocity and emotional availability go a long way.

THREE

RADICAL CLARITY

HONESTY IS LOVING, CLARITY IS CONSIDERATE, AND communication is key. I carry these three things close to my heart as I navigate the complexities of being in relationships. When we choose to be in relationships with people, we also choose to be loving, considerate, and clear in our communication. I know that doesn't always pan out, but we do our best with the tools that we have at the time. I wish I had learned the value of creating healthy connections earlier in life—the beauty in clear communication and saying what I wanted and needed upfront instead of beating around the bush. Fear and being in healthy relationships don't often mix well. If we are scared to show up, we usually fear being vulnerable, too. Vulnerability is how trust thrives in relationships. When we say yes to bringing new people into our lives or deepening an existing relationship, there's an assumption of trust. We trust that the relationship we're entering will be good for and to us. We trust that honesty, consideration, and openness will be valued. We trust that we are in this together. Over the years, I've realized that to have thriving relationships, I need and want to be on the same page as the people I share my life with.

In 2024, I started practicing radical clarity not just with others but with myself. Why? Because I realized I'd been lying for too long. I'd fallen deep into the trap of overcommitting and overextending to keep the peace and not rock the boat. Going along to get along and people-pleasing should've been my middle name. I wanted so badly to be well-received, we all do, it's human nature. When it came to friendship in particular, I found myself not wanting to ruffle feathers or inconvenience anyone, because saving face and being a good friend—the one people could call whenever and count on for everything—meant more than how I really felt inside. I didn't want anyone to be mad at me, ever. Because God forbid, someone didn't like me or want me around anymore. But when it finally came down to being honest with myself, it became more and more clear that I didn't want to be deemed good if that meant I'd have to leave myself behind. I'd much rather be the villain in someone else's story for letting them down, than a good girl for abandoning myself.

As time went on, I became more secure in my ability to be truthful about how I could or couldn't show up. In all that I do, I want to be truthful and clear. That requires being open and honest. Having clarity changed the game for me. My communication style started to become more mindful and intentional. Before saying yes to anything, I tapped into myself. I asked myself questions like, *Do you have the space for this? Do you actually want to do this? Why are you saying yes?*

Asking myself these questions was a part of my soul work. Self-check-ins became my compass on the journey to radical clarity, guiding me to make decisions that truly aligned with my values and desires. Saying yes out of obligation or fear of disappointing others was not serving me or creating relationships rooted in authenticity or intention.

EXAMPLES OF HOW I PUT
THIS INTO PRACTICE:

- Work commitments: Before accepting new projects or extra responsibilities at work, I asked myself if I had the emotional bandwidth and time to commit without sacrificing my mental health. I respectfully declined or renegotiated time lines to protect my well-being if the answer was no.

- Social invitations: Instead of agreeing to attend social events out of guilt or to avoid disappointing friends, I checked in with my energy levels. If I felt drained, I opted out and was honest about why I needed rest, building relationships based on honesty rather than obligation.

- Helping others: When friends or family reached out for help, I paused to consider if I was truly in a position to support them without compromising my well-being. Sometimes, this meant offering alternative solutions rather than stretching myself too thin.

Self-check-ins are the quiet moments that reshape our relationships in profound ways. When we pause and ask ourselves what we can truly offer, we show up with honesty, allowing others to trust that our yes means yes and our no is filled with care. This authenticity builds stronger connections, where mutual consideration can prosper because everyone knows where they stand. Having our friendship foundations rooted in clarity allows the truth to become the bridge between us.

Without inner reflection, we risk overcommitting and slowly draining ourselves. Resentment begins to simmer, frustration grows, and relationships suffer under the weight of unspoken exhaustion. I had to realize that no one was asking me to overcommit. I was doing that to myself. Self-check-ins are a protection against this. They remind us to give from a place of fullness, ensuring that we show up for others in ways that feel good for us, too, keeping resentment at bay.

When I started being real with myself and honest about my capacity, I was unknowingly creating space for vulnerability. Being honest about our boundaries invites others to do the same. It opens up room for deeper connections and more compassionate conversations. Telling the truth about what we can and cannot do is a nudge to remember that we do not need or have to pretend. When we are clear about our capacity, our connections become more meaningful, aligned, and deeply rooted in reciprocity and respect.

Clarity came to the surface when I started saying yes when it felt right for me instead of when it felt like a duty that I was dreading before it even happened. Shifting in this way allowed me to honor my own needs and boundaries, which, in turn, deepened my relationships and fostered a sense of inner peace. Nobody wants the people in their lives to show up half-assed or with trepidation. Something else that started to make itself very apparent to me is that people, including myself, don't like being manipulated or lied to. So when we agree to something that we deep down do not have the space or desire to do, we are participating in a form of manipulation and deceit, not just to others but also ourselves. And yes, that sounds intense, but for me, it's true. I had to start looking at myself and making major changes. I am not a liar, deceiver, or manipulator, but in those moments of saying yes when I wanted to say no, I was cosplaying all those things. Not moving in our truth or authenticity will take us out of character even when we don't intend to—and I was abandoning myself in the process. It was a lose-lose situation that only I could change. The more I practiced radical clarity, the more I noticed a profound transformation within myself that cultivated self-respect, compassionate honesty, and authentic connection. When navigating this terrain, I had to realize that it wasn't about being perfect or pleasing everyone—it was about being real with myself and others and finding freedom in that truth.

A few summers ago, I took a last-minute trip to New York with my oldest daughter to see my friend L. She was booked for a big photo shoot and wanted us to come.

Her text came in at five p.m., and at eight p.m., we were on the train headed to Penn Station. Before I said that we'd be coming, I did a self-check-in. I knew myself well enough then to honestly ask myself if I wanted to go out of state again. I'd been traveling back and forth for weeks. Was I tired? Did I have enough enthusiasm to support and celebrate my friend in the way she deserved? Would this trip be cup-filling or draining? Before committing to L, I sat and took some deep breaths. I told myself to answer honestly. I reminded myself that L would not be mad at me if the answer were no, that our friendship would not be on the line if I couldn't show up. I had to remember that I was safe with her and that our relationship would stay solid regardless of my decision. The answer ended up aligning with taking the trip, I had the space. So my daughter and I went and enjoyed thirty-six hours in New York.

That felt like a lightbulb moment for me. A wave of gratitude washed over me. I'd finally started checking in and getting clear at the moment and not after the fact. The pausing, the presence with myself, and the honesty that emerged felt like proof of healing. I wasn't going through the motions or agreeing out of habit or people-pleasing. Tuning in to my needs and desires, listening to myself, and checking in with myself first and foremost felt empowering. Saying yes or no became less about rejecting or appeasing others and more about the practice of honoring us both. I wanted to stop showing up for people with half of myself. Pouring from a vessel that is bone dry is impossible—literally. I realized that by being honest with myself, I was creating more freedom for the things that mattered. The more I practiced this, the easier it became to set boundaries and make aligned decisions. Being honest with ourselves means we must look at and evaluate whether we're being generous or overextending—whether we're acting out of truthfulness and integrity, or simply trying to fulfill the obligation of being seen as "good" and likable.

Radical clarity and compassionate honesty are a work in progress, but it's a worthy shift. It makes life feel more authentic and less cluttered with expectations and assumptions.

At the heart of every meaningful relationship lies the responsibility to communicate openly and truthfully. However, in a world where we've grown accustomed to the mantra of "not owing" anyone anything, we've blurred the lines between healthy boundaries and avoidance. Building responsible relationships requires honesty because it fosters trust, deepens understanding, and builds a foundation of mutual respect. When we are honest, we honor our own truth and create a safe space for others to express theirs. This level of authenticity paves the way for deeper and more sturdy connections.

For example, instead of brushing off a friend's repeated cancellations with a polite *"It's fine,"* you might say, *"I've noticed we've had to reschedule a lot, and I value our time together. Is everything okay on your end?"* This kind of curious communication opens the door for honesty, acknowledging your feelings, and for them to share their truth. Perhaps they've been overwhelmed and are afraid to say so, or maybe they hadn't realized how their actions were impacting you. Either way, your openness sets the tone for a conversation that is grounded in care and mutual respect, strengthening the relationship rather than fracturing it.

Such honesty prevents resentment and allows us to address things head-on rather than sweeping them under the rug with pacifying yeses when we want to say *no, not this time,* or *not today.* As someone who prioritized silence over speaking up, I've come to value the beauty that compassion, transparency, and honesty can bring to our bonds with others. I had to learn how to zoom out and past my fear of being hurt or causing harm, feeling rejected and possibly misunderstood. Having the space to see that truth and vulnerability are the glue that holds relationships together, ensuring resilience and endurance in the face of challenges.

Through my many ebbs and flows, it's become clear that transparency is a courageous act of love, even if it feels hard and uncomfortable. It takes immense courage to confront our fears of being misunderstood or causing hurt. It takes self-awareness to be introspective and non-avoidant. Cultivating healthy relationships needs head-on intentional work. The alternative erodes trust, weakens connections, and can lead to far greater harm. Telling the truth about our capacity and doing our best to stay empathetic when doing so is sacred. Going along to get along may feel like a shield of protection, but it's not. The lack of clarity and truth sharpens the edges of doubt and insecurity.

In all my relationships, being clear and honest has demonstrated consideration, care, and basic decency. For instance, when a close friend kept inviting me to late-night dinners after I had my third daughter, I found myself constantly making excuses instead of admitting that those plans just didn't work for me anymore. Eventually, I decided to be honest. I told her, "I miss our time together, but evenings are so tough for me right now with the kids' schedules and my own energy levels. Could we plan a coffee date instead, a FaceTime tea and talk session, or maybe a weekend brunch?"

I felt vulnerable sharing that, worried she'd think I wasn't invested in our friendship because of motherhood; but instead, she responded with kindness. She admitted she'd been feeling out of sync and that her life was changing in other ways. She also apologized for not considering that my life changed during parenthood—I was not expecting that. Her acknowledgment, compassion, and grace brought me to tears. I apologized, too, for not being upfront with her out of fear of rejection. That conversation deepened our bond, and we found a rhythm that worked for both of us by putting intentional time on the calendar for each other every quarter. That moment of honesty allowed her to meet me where I was, and vice versa. It also reminded me that connection is possible when we show up as our authentic and unpolished selves.

The relationships in my life where open communication is a priority have thrived on mutual respect and understanding. Even in cases where the truth led to difficult decisions or endings, a sense of integrity was maintained. Being able to show up and truly listen, witness, love, and cradle those I care about feels fundamentally different when I am in a space of autonomy. Many of us are conditioned to go with the flow, to do things out of obligation, or to prove our worth by overextending ourselves. Reflecting on my friendships and relationships over the past five years, I've realized that it becomes challenging to show up intentionally for the people I love when I don't feel fully and wholly myself. If we lack autonomy—spiritually, physically, or emotionally—we might struggle to hold deep and meaningful space. I often say that *when we heal ourselves, we heal each other,* and understanding this is particularly resonant in my life. I've done so much healing work, and while healing is never truly complete, I now feel that I have enough space to be intentional and purposeful in how I show up in my relationships and friendships—even if it's just for a quick trip to New York to see a friend.

Reflections

- In what areas of your life do you feel the most resistance to practicing radical clarity and compassionate honesty? What fears or concerns are holding you back?

- How does practicing radical clarity in your communication help you feel more aligned with your true self? In what ways does it reduce or increase the mental clutter of expectations and assumptions?

- What relationships in your life could benefit from more compassionate honesty? How might this shift transform these connections and create deeper authenticity?

- What changes do you envision making when you think about living a life less cluttered by expectations? How can radical clarity support you in this process?

- What does radical clarity mean to you personally? How do you see it evolving as you continue practicing it with yourself and others?

Sometimes, the most loving thing we can do for ourselves is let things fall into place after falling apart.

FOUR

WHEN THINGS UNRAVEL

THE MOMENTS WHEN LIFE COMPELS US TO TRULY CON-
front ourselves—who we are, what we're doing, and
who we're sharing our time with—are some of the
most pivotal reckonings we'll face in our healing. Despite
being uncomfortable, and even daunting, it's necessary to
zoom in and look at what's in front of us. There's no side-
stepping this. I know because I've tried multiple times to
avoid accountability, discomfort, and the overwhelm that
comes with facing my relationships head-on. Specifically
the ones that were no longer working, aligned, or healthy.

The truth of the matter is that reflection is mandatory, sooner rather than later. Thriving in our relationships and building a circle of closeness that feels aligned and intentional requires honesty. We all need and deserve community, yet many of us struggle with finding our people. Shrinking myself to fit in was my go-to. Like most of us, I wanted to be loved and liked. And I thought in order to be welcomed by others, I needed to be small, contained, and well-behaved so that I didn't cause too much disruption in their life. I thought ease meant being agreeable. But eventually I learned that I had a choice in how I showed up and who I shared space with. Too often, we move through life as fragments of ourselves. Yearning for acceptance from people who don't fully see us and may never be able to. Finding our people invites us to be willing to stand tall, even when it means going against the grain, making some waves, and sinking the damn boat that we've been trying to keep steady. We must show up unapologetically in our lives, with or without someone else's willingness to be a witness. What I've come to know over the years is that the company I keep must be open to creating emotional intimacy. And the only way that can be done is through vulnerability. Being vulnerable is our compass to connection. Guiding us to deepen our relationships that foster healthy closeness and reevaluate the ones that can no longer—or never did—hold the fullness of who we are. When our connections are aligned, clarity emerges and authenticity flourishes.

As we evolve, our needs and desires do, too. Sometimes this truth is the hardest to reconcile. There will be moments when we think our decades-long friendships are a forever thing and then a shift, big or small, happens and that thought no longer rings true. The reckoning is, we grow together in certain seasons, or we drift apart. This is natural even if it feels wrong or leaves us feeling crappy about the shedding that might be on the horizon. I've also come to realize that emotional intimacy is absolutely necessary in our relationships. For me, that means feeling seen without the shadow of judgment hanging over me. It is in emotionally safe relationships that we experience profound moments of vulnerability. In my experience, that is where trust and closeness are born. And during times of conflict, we're quick to find out if we'll be embraced in our raw, honest, and imperfect selves or not. Many of my past relationships lacked that foundation of healthy emotional connection. Emotional intimacy creates a space to let down our guard and trust that our hearts are safe with someone else, but for years I didn't have that. Why? Because I was more attached to the idea and potential of people than to who they truly showed me they were.

A few years ago, I had a friendship of more than ten years dissolve, and to this day I am still shocked. There was a point in time where I thought we were unshakable. I knew with my whole being that we were solid and I was the one friend who'd be standing with her at the end of the day. Let's call her Kia. Together, we had countless conversations about staying clear, open, and compassionate with each other. One summer, Kia and I were in my kitchen and I was crying into her shoulder. It had been an emotional year for both of us when it came to relationships. I remember us saying that no matter what, we would always do our due diligence to prioritize honest and healthy communication in our friendship. We'd grown a lot together over the years, from women in their early twenties to wiser women in their thirties. I thought we knew and understood each other well, but looking back, I realize that sometimes even the foundations we feel are the strongest can crack in places we can't see. Life has a way of testing the bonds we have, and though Kia and I promised to stay clear and compassionate, something shifted. I began to notice subtle changes—conversations that once felt effortless became tense, and the openness we prided ourselves on slowly gave way to guardedness. The emotional closeness that felt unbreakable started to unravel in ways I couldn't fully grasp then. It was like we were drifting apart, even as we held on to the idea of who we used to be. Then one day, I stopped hearing from her—and to be honest, behind my sadness, I also felt relieved. Relieved that I didn't have to worry about where I stood with her, she made it clear by leaving my texts on READ, unfollowing me on social media, and forwarding calls to voicemail. I had believed our connection was built to withstand anything, but in reality I was holding on to a version of us that no longer existed.

Ultimately, it didn't matter how much I cherished Kia as one of my closest friends. The years we spent together and the deep conversations we had about staying aligned couldn't hold up against the reality that we had grown apart. I had to face the hard truth that things had changed—we were no longer able to truly see or hear each other. As much as I wanted to honor our connection by having a conversation that would bring clarity and closure, she refused. And I had to accept that by letting the friendship unravel, despite how much it hurt. Being left in the dark wasn't just painful—it was disorienting. Yet, when I looked back, I saw how many signs I had chosen to ignore, brushing them off as "just the way she is." I stayed because I was afraid of being cut off. I had seen her discard people so effortlessly, quicker than I could blink, but I convinced myself we were different. I believed our bond was stronger and that she would never treat me the way she treated others. But that illusion crumbled, and suddenly, I found myself on the receiving end of the same coldness I had witnessed repeatedly.

Still, I held on, clinging to the sisterhood I thought we had. My kids called her "Auntie." How could I let that go? So I stayed quiet when things hurt. I let small things slide to keep the peace, convincing myself that silence was better than conflict. I walked on eggshells, hoping that staying calm and loving would soothe whatever storms were swirling in her spirit. But in doing so, I was betraying my own boundaries. I'd become tired of sacrificing my voice to keep the fragile balance of a friendship that was crumbling around me. The more I suppressed my feelings, the clearer it became: I was compromising my well-being for a friendship that never felt truly reciprocal.

A lot of us risk our inner peace to be in connection with people because we crave belonging, even when it costs us pieces of ourselves. We bend, adjust, and silence our truth to fit into the comfort zones of others that were never meant for us. We ignore the red flags, telling ourselves that loyalty means endurance, even when it hurts. However, if I've learned anything over the years it has been this: True friendship shouldn't make us feel small, timid, or dismissed. It should be the place where our spirit feels at ease, safe, and seen, exactly as we are. Sometimes we stay in relationships longer than we should because we're afraid of the void their absence might leave. We convince ourselves that the pain of staying is somehow more bearable than the pain of letting go. But eventually, we come to understand that clinging to what no longer aligns with us only delays our growth and healing. At the end of day, I had to remind myself that true sisterhood doesn't weaponize silence or encourage self-betrayal—it invites honesty and love even when it's uncomfortable.

The heartbreak of that loss was something I could never have prepared for, not in a million years. But that pain taught me a crucial lesson: If we want deeper and healthier relationships, we must be willing to make the tough adjustments. We must be open and vulnerable. It starts with acknowledging what—and who—is no longer in alignment with our growth, including parts of our former selves. Kia and I were in different seasons and that was hard for us to be honest about, even though we vowed to always be.

Reflecting on that time, I can see how she could only meet me as far as she'd come in her healing. I have grace for her because so many of us were never taught how to build healthy relationships—I know I wasn't. I grew up in a household where my voice wasn't heard and conflict wasn't handled in emotionally healthy ways. In adulthood, this fed my tendency to stay small and quiet even when I was crumbling inside. I tiptoed around issues with Kia because I didn't know what would set her off or cause her to stop talking to me. But I can also see how she would have felt the same way about me. The healing space I was in wasn't where she was yet, and that can be intimidating. In dealing with the abrupt friendship ending, I had to make peace with the fact that love isn't always enough. I loved her deeply but knew our friendship was over, and at the time was beyond repair. Relationships take more than just proximity or affection. They require willingness, openness, and space to grow, which is something we'd lost even though we cared for each other deeply.

It took me a long time to recover from that friendship breakup. Being ghosted by her cut deep. I had to force myself to remember that healthy relationships aren't some elusive dream meant for just a lucky few. Deep down, I knew I was worthy of relationships that were nurturing and kind, but this experience made me second-guess. However, as disappointing as her absence was, I knew we were on different paths and it was time for us to go our separate ways. Because I was met with silence, I grieved on my own and had a lot of talks with my husband on how this could be possible. Nevertheless, I sent her love every time she crossed my mind, and decided that I was not going to chase behind anyone who was avoiding me. A part of me wanted to harden my heart and not let anyone new in when this happened. But I knew that was my fear and hurt talking—and that adopting that defense mechanism would not serve me. Ultimately, I didn't want to block my blessings or new gifts of friendship and closeness.

On this journey to creating healthier connections with people, I had to start naming what I wanted and needed in friendship. I knew I wanted friends willing to be honest, even when it wasn't easy, and who could hold space for my joys and struggles. I needed friendships where vulnerability was welcomed, where we could have tough conversations without fear of rejection. I wanted connections rooted in mutual respect, where my boundaries were honored and my feelings were valued. I longed for relationships where we could celebrate and witness each other's growth even when it meant growing in different directions, and where the effort to stay connected was always reciprocated. In naming these desires, I began to see the kinds of friendships that truly nurtured my soul and let go of those that didn't. It became increasingly evident that lasting relationships need intention, care, and trust from everyone involved. These things don't just appear—they're built, nurtured, and require a mutual effort. We can create healthy and clear connections with others, but only if we're willing to be honest about our lives and whom we allow to share space with us.

Through all of this, I learned many things. Here are a few of them:

1. Set clear boundaries early on: Healthy friendships thrive on mutual respect, and that starts with setting boundaries. Let your friends know what feels comfortable and uncomfortable for you. Whether it's about your time, emotional capacity, or personal space, boundaries balance relationships and help prevent resentment.

2. Communicate openly and honestly: The foundation of any strong friendship is communication. It's important to be vulnerable, even when it's uncomfortable. If something bothers you, address it. Don't wait until you're at your wit's end. Honest conversations build trust and deepen the connection.

3. Prioritize mutual support: Healthy friendships require a balance of give and take. Reciprocity is sacred. It's not about keeping score but ensuring that both parties feel valued and supported.

4. Respect each other's growth: As we grow and change, so do our friendships. It's important to honor each other's evolution, even if it means the dynamic of your relationship shifts. Be willing to give each other room to grow while maintaining your connection's core. A healthy friendship allows for individuality while still holding space for togetherness.

5. Make time for intentional connection: Life gets busy, but maintaining a friendship requires effort. Making time for each other helps strengthen the bond. Being intentional, through

the ebbs and flows, shows that the relationship is valued and you're invested in keeping it alive.

The truth is, people are beautifully complex, constantly reshaping themselves for different reasons. For those of us who crave growth and emotional expansion, staying stagnant isn't an option. When we give ourselves the grace and permission to evolve through the seasons of life, we stay self-aware and become more aligned with what we truly want. That creates space to pay attention to when our values shift or our communication styles change. These shifts are an invitation to home in on what we thought we wanted and get curious about what may no longer fit. Who we were when we met someone years ago may not be who we are today—and there's beauty in that, even if it feels unsettling.

I was caught in a cycle of choosing to perpetuate unhealthy cycles with the same people. Naming this was a wake-up call for me. The beautiful thing about growth, even when we experience its growing pains, is that in order to bloom, we must shed and wilt. We cannot hold on to the way things are if we want different results. I knew that if I wanted the deep, meaningful relationships I longed for, I had to start letting go—cutting things and habits loose that I knew were keeping me stuck in quicksand. Making the tough choices to not only deepen my connections with others but also to nurture the relationship I had with myself was the only way for me to plant newness in fertile soil. After all, I was the common thread. A major part of my growth was looking at my own reflection and saying, *Girl, it might be you. If you want different, you must be willing to show up and do different.* There comes a time when we have to start doing self-check-ins and looking inward, asking ourselves not only how we can evolve and grow, but what loose ends we need to cut to see ourselves more clearly.

For those of us who are intentionally working to become better, we know this all too well. Sometimes, it *is* us. Sometimes, we have to be the ones leading the change, whether we like it or not—it's our responsibility. I've learned this lesson the hard way more than a few times. When I decided to prioritize my well-being and truly show up for myself, the dynamics in my life shifted dramatically. Some relationships thrived, while others, like the one I shared earlier, faded. But I quickly learned that healing and growth are inseparable from the company we keep. The people around us can either help us rise or hold us back.

Reflections

- What relationships in your life currently support your healing and growth? How do these connections make you feel empowered and aligned with your values?

- Reflect on a relationship that has faded or shifted as you've grown. What lessons did you learn from that experience, and how did it impact you?

- In what ways have you been responsible for leading change in your relationships? How did taking that responsibility affect you, and what was the outcome?

- How do you ensure the people around you contribute to your growth and well-being? What boundaries or practices do you put in place to protect your peace?

- Think about a time when you had to let go of a friendship or relationship for your own healing. How did that decision feel in the moment, and what insights have you gained since then?

FIVE

CHECK IN WITH YOURSELF

N 2022, I STARTED DOING QUARTERLY SELF-CHECK-INS—they've helped me deepen into the radical clarity that I've been exploring. In order to stay clear and aligned with myself and the people around me, I had to tap into home base first. Me—I am home base. Coasting through life without introspection is risky and it keeps us stuck in our own bubble, out of touch, and going through the motions. This is not fruitful for our connections. It also reduces our access to self-awareness. When I feel at ease with myself, my relationships thrive. Some people do not agree with this, but I strongly believe that to be in healthy and intentional relationships with others, we have to be in healthy and intentional relationship with ourselves. My relationships suffered when I was out of alignment with myself. I didn't realize it initially. I thought life's stressors and busyness just swallowed me up. But the truth was, I wasn't showing up for myself and it spilled into how I showed up for others. Small things started to pile up—missed calls I didn't return, conversations I half-listened to, and plans I cancelled at the last minute. My people could feel it, and honestly, so could I. There was one moment that shook me awake. A dear friend gently said, "I feel like I've been losing you lately." Her words stung, not because they were harsh, but because they were true. I had been neglecting myself—ignoring my own needs, pushing through exhaustion, and trying to pour from an empty cup. In doing so, I was not surprised when the people closest to me voiced that they felt neglected and disconnected.

That's when I realized alignment isn't just about self-care—it's about self-respect. I started being deliberate in how I showed up for myself. I set boundaries with my time, gave myself permission to rest, and made space for the things that nourished me. As I watered my roots and took care of home base, my friendships started rehydrating. I was able to be more present, clear, and compassionate—

not just for them but for myself, too. When I wasn't feeling aligned, everyone could tell—my husband, my kids, and my friends. We often think that the load we're carrying isn't visible, but it is. Self-check-ins play a huge role in my well-being. I can take inventory of how full or empty my cup is. Putting words to what we want and need is crucial to being in community with others. When we prioritize our well-being, our relationships feel different in the best way. We can be reminded that how we care for ourselves echoes how we care for others. Alignment is necessary. It's an act of love, extended inward and outward.

Life can be hard. We all have responsibilities to tend to. It's easy to get lost in our own worlds and forget about the rest. However, being in mindful relationships with my chosen family and friends is something I did not want to take for granted. So I started to pay closer attention to how I was feeling so that I could address life's tender moments and rough edges with care. Honestly, being able to communicate with the company I was keeping meant a lot to me, and I realized that when I was neglecting my needs or letting my boundaries slide, irritation would quietly build, impacting how I interacted with others.

Here are a few things you can try:

1. Set aside time for solo reflection: Choose a quiet time each week to check in with yourself.

Ask, *How am I feeling emotionally, mentally, and physically?* and *Am I honoring my boundaries?*

2. **Create a personal alignment list:** Write down your core values and periodically reflect on whether your actions and relationships are in harmony with those values. This practice can help you recognize when you're out of alignment and what adjustments might be needed.

3. **Write down your thoughts and feelings:** Regularly reflect on how your relationships impact you. Are they supportive, draining, or somewhere in between? Use questions like, *What do I need from my friendships right now?* or *Am I clearly communicating my needs and boundaries?*

4. **Pencil yourself in:** Make time each quarter for a deeper self-reflection. Ask yourself what's going well, where you feel out of sync, and if any relationships need more attention or recalibration.

5. **Reassess your energy commitments:** List your current relationships or social commitments and evaluate whether they are uplifting or exhausting. Are there any that no longer align with who you are becoming? Be honest.

6. Practice intentional conversations: Be proactive when you notice tension or misalignment in a relationship. Approach the person with kindness and clarity, and share what you've noticed about yourself. Use "I" statements to express your needs or concerns, like, "I've been feeling overwhelmed lately and need more downtime to recharge."

7. Boundaries audit: Reflect on your current boundaries. Are there places where they've become too loose or rigid? What boundaries could you implement to protect your peace and stay true to yourself? Write them down and practice reinforcing them in small steps.

Taking the time to reconnect with my core values helps me show up in my relationships with more patience, empathy, and honesty. My friendships started to shift for the better when I stopped ignoring myself and instead started taking inventory. I've noticed over the years that some people value clarity just as much as I do. Some of my relationships flourished wildly after implementing more introspection because I could show up with clarity. A goal of mine was to move away from surface-level interactions to deeper, more meaningful connections. The more I checked in with myself, the more I could recognize what I truly needed from the people in my life—and, just as important, what I had to offer them.

Self-check-ins are a way to take our emotional temperature, giving us pause and time to ask: What and who still feels good and grounding? And what—or who—no longer aligns with where I'm headed? Most of the time, the answers I got back invited me to dive deeper into my feelings and capacity. It wasn't always about who wasn't in alignment with me but how I was aligning with others. Taking emotional inventory is an act of mindfulness and honesty that we all need more of, and I want to encourage you all to start thinking about doing the same. Since I began practicing this regularly, without the weight of guilt or shame, my relationships—especially my friendships—have evolved and become more open. Approaching the company we keep with curiosity and compassion makes all the difference, allowing us to nurture genuine, safe, and emotionally regulating connections. These moments of reflection allow us to assess whether our relationships support us in healthy, meaningful ways.

But here's the catch: being honest with ourselves about what is or isn't working can be uncomfortable. Some of us avoid vulnerability because we fear we'll be misunderstood, unheard, or rejected. It's a natural fear, but we risk stagnation when we keep those feelings inside. Our needs go unspoken, and we continue in relationships that may no longer align with who we've become.

A few years ago, I was working with one of my *Writing to Heal* clients—let's call her Sarah—who was facing this exact struggle. She was terrified of damaging a long-standing friendship that had been an important part of her life for over a decade. Sarah had evolved over the years—her values, priorities, and even how she wanted to spend her time had shifted. But her friend hadn't changed in the same way. They were in two different seasons of life, and my client mentioned that it was hard to ignore that they were no longer on the same path. She came to me for help in processing these feelings on the page in hopes that she would gain more confidence, new tools, and clearer language to have a much-needed talk with her friend.

Sarah shared with me that her friendship needs had shifted dramatically. She craved deeper conversations, more shared growth, and a mutual support system but didn't know how to broach the conversation. The last thing Sarah wanted to do was upset her friend or make her feel bad. Sarah felt stuck. She didn't want to lose the friendship, but she also couldn't ignore her growing frustration and emotional exhaustion from trying to maintain a connection that no longer felt fulfilling.

As I sat and listened to Sarah, it was clear that the underlying issue was that she was terrified of the friendship possibly being over. I could tell that this friend meant a lot to Sarah and that she loved her dearly, but she lacked clarity about what she wanted and how to express those desires. One of the first things Sarah said to me when we hopped on Zoom was: *"Alex, change scares me. Sometimes, I would rather not know what's coming and stay in the dark than be transparent and risk being hurt."* This is where self-check-ins can support us, especially if we are open to being forthcoming about where we are and what we want.

Once Sarah was finished sharing her thoughts with me, I asked her to write down the answer to this question: *Do I want to continue being friends with this person?*

I had her save her answer until the end of our four-week session. During that time, we did a lot of processing on the page, lots of voice note journaling, and a lot of sharing about what was important for that season of Sarah's life. When it comes to the relationships we're in, clarity is key.

So many of us have experienced a version of this from one side or the other. Being scared to address our truth keeps us tethered to people, places, and things we've long outgrown. Honesty requires us to do the hard thing, have the difficult conversation, and sit in the discomfort that will likely arise. Sarah's fear of having an open conversation with her friend stemmed from her desire to avoid conflict and rejection. But through her self-check-ins, she realized she was sabotaging her well-being and stifling the friendship by avoiding vulnerability.

After our four weeks were over, Sarah was ready to take the bold step of initiating a conversation with her friend. She approached it with empathy and honesty, sharing how she'd changed and how her friendship needs had evolved. To her surprise, the conversation went better than expected. Though her friend initially struggled to understand, she eventually expressed gratitude for Sarah's openness. I was happy to learn that they were able to redefine their friendship in a way that honored both of their needs. And while their dynamic shifted, the relationship continued in a healthier, more authentic way. Sarah also shared her answer about their friendship with me from the start of our session. Her response was, *Yes, I want to continue being friends.* The lesson here is that vulnerability—especially in relationships—requires courage, which is often the key to growth. When we avoid being transparent because we fear the outcome, we deny ourselves and others the chance to adjust, evolve, and meet each other where we truly are.

In our self-check-ins, we must ask, *"Am I being honest with myself about what I need?"* and, just as important, *"Am I being honest with the people in my life about what I need from them?"* These questions may lead to tough conversations, but they may also open the door to deeper understanding, better alignment, and more fulfilling connections. By embracing these delicate moments of vulnerability, like

Sarah did, we give ourselves the space to mature—and invite others to do the same alongside us. Self-reflection gives us a deeper understanding of our role in our relationships. Sometimes, it's not about what others are doing wrong but about what and how we need to adjust within ourselves. It was beautiful to see my client come to this realization. Ultimately, she understood that unspoken assumptions or unresolved feelings within can shape how we view our connections and what we expect from others.

When we start examining our emotional landscape by checking in with ourselves more frequently, we can show up in our relationships with more clarity and compassion instead of expecting others to fulfill needs that we haven't first addressed within ourselves.

Reflections

- What unmet needs have you recently become aware of, and how can you take responsibility for addressing them within yourself?

- How can you nurture your emotional well-being before seeking support from others so that you can show up more fully in your relationships?

- In the past, how have you projected your unaddressed emotions onto others, and what steps can you take to break this cycle?

- What practices help you check in with yourself regularly to better understand your emotions and needs?

- How can you communicate your needs to others more clearly without expecting them to fulfill or fix what's unresolved within you?

SIX

SACRED SUPPORT

A T THE TOP OF 2024, MY HUSBAND'S FATHER SUDDENLY passed away. Getting the call from Ryan's sister was gut-wrenching. *"Where is Ryan? Is he with you? You need to hold him. I got some bad news."* I remember my husband crying out with heartache after asking his sister, *"Is Daddy dead?"* She said, in almost a whisper, *"Yes."* I will never forget the look on his face. I could see his heart shatter in real time. Tears streamed down his cheeks as he screamed, *"No, no, no."* The most painful sound I'd ever heard came from him that day. It was devastating. I remember feeling hopeless and not knowing what to do or say. I remember crying as I followed behind him while he paced and paced and paced. I remember him saying, *"Babe, don't follow me,"* as he retreated to the basement. He wanted to be alone—he needed to be. So I stopped in my tracks, honoring his request, watching his pain flood into the space with each step. I wanted to hold him and make it all better, but there is no "all better" when your daddy dies. And in order to process this very painful thing, he didn't need me hovering. What he wanted and needed from me was space to think and wrap his mind around how his life just changed. The days to follow were hazy and blurry. They seemed to move at a snail's pace and Usain Bolt speed all at once. It was disorienting and dizzying. My heart broke many times over for Ryan and his siblings. The grief was soul-shredding, murky, and thick enough to cut through. It left remnants of salt in the corners of our eyes and on our pillowcases for days on end. There were so many tears that our home flooded and turned into the Dead Sea—and there was nowhere to go. All we could do was float through the waters of what loss had left behind. No one prepares us for this kind of loss. At first, it can feel like you'll never figure out how to navigate the crushing weight of grief or how to support someone you love when they're in the deepest pit of sorrow. No one tells us how tender and emotional it is to do your best in supporting the person experiencing the loss. Time doesn't heal wounds like this. Attempting to be comforting with words doesn't land and often feels hollow. Life as we knew it was no longer. Everything stretched, slowed, and bent under the heaviness of sadness.

A couple of weeks after Ryan's dad died, a good friend of mine texted to me, *I've been thinking about you. It's hard supporting a spouse who is going through such a big loss. How are you?* I read her message over and over again, unsure how to respond. I felt guilty for being asked about my well-being. After all, I wasn't the one who needed consoling. In my mind, my husband was the person who needed to be held and cared for, not me. I replied to her, saying, *I'm fine, I guess. I haven't really thought about it.* She texted back shortly after, saying, *You should start thinking about it. We can't show up fully for those we love without showing up for ourselves. I love you both. I am praying for you all.*

I needed that reminder so badly. It was at that moment that gratitude washed over me. Her message was proof that the women I'd chosen to keep close were exactly who I needed during that season of my life. They were my mirror on the days I lost sight of who I was. Being supported with love and compassion reminded me that I was allowed to feel all of the swirling emotions that were coming up—it was okay for me to be hurting, too. Welcoming that instead of shying away helped me release an exhale I didn't even know I was holding in. Going into support mode for my husband was an honor. I had the capacity to show up 110 percent, but I'd been so consumed with his grief that I forgot my own heart needed tending to as well. The gentle reminder I got from my sister-friend over text gave me permission to start acknowledging my feelings—not just as a supportive partner but as a person navigating my own sea of emotions. I realized that being strong for Ryan didn't have to mean ignoring the sadness I was experiencing. And while I wasn't the one who had lost a parent, I was grieving—grieving for the man I love, for his siblings, for our children, for the sudden change in our lives, and for the weight of holding so much pain all at once. I hadn't allowed myself to feel it, to process it, or to even consider that I had my own sorrow to face. But in that simple text exchange from a good friend, I was reminded that self-nurturing is not inconsiderate, it's essential.

This is why it's important for us to surround ourselves with people who can bear witness to us, even when we've turned away from our reflection. The nudge I got to tune in and be present with myself reflected the kind of support that goes beyond platitudes. We didn't need anything surface level from anyone. We wanted people around who were willing to go deep with us if and when we needed it. My friend showed me care simply by reminding me that I matter. Her words helped me recognize that I couldn't put myself on the back burner. Ryan needed the version of me that was full and present, and for me to do that, I had to add myself to the equation without feeling unworthy or guilty.

Having friendships that remind you to check in with yourself amid emotional chaos and grief is invaluable. It's a testament to the power of what can unfold when intentional relationships take root. The company we keep isn't defined by the title of "friend" but by the deliberate actions it takes to be one. For me, true friendship means being able to hold up a mirror for our loved ones when they're too weary to do it themselves—and that's exactly what my friend did for me.

I will never forget that moment or the deep gratitude I felt for her words and for the community of women who stood by me during such a tender time. I'm proud that my small circle of friends understands the delicate balance between giving to others and giving to yourself. We've come to know each other so well that we can remind one another to breathe, take up space, and weep when needed. To be seen at our most vulnerable and still have people show up with grace and love is life altering. In being seen, and being reminded that I deserve to be, I found strength—not only to support Ryan, but also to experience what it means to take up space in my own healing and processing.

As we all know, grief doesn't come with instructions. There's no blueprint for how to show up for someone when the person they love is gone. There were moments when all I could do was be present in Ryan's moments of silence, respect his need for solitude, and be ready when he needed me. We moved through some days like ghosts, clinging to pieces of our routine in hopes they'd provide some sense of normalcy. But nothing was normal anymore for Ryan. Both of his parents were gone, and he was entering a new chapter. Watching him learn what it means to live and love without the people who gave him life has been admirable. I do not take being a witness to his pain for granted at all. It is an honor to welcome the vulnerability of others, especially my life partner's. Through all of this, I learned that sometimes love means letting someone shatter, allowing them to feel the depth of their pain, even when every part of you wants to reach out and make it better. Sometimes, the most loving thing we can do for someone is be a compassionate observer to their suffering instead of trying to fix it.

Grief, I discovered, is something that clamors to be felt. It's raw, loud, and unfiltered. It demands space, patience, and acceptance. There are no quick fixes, no easy answers. It strips you bare, leaving you to find new ways to exist in a world that's now fundamentally altered. In the aftermath, we weren't the same people we were before. Loss changes you. It rearranges the landscape of your heart, and you begin to understand that healing is not about returning to who you once were—it's about learning how to carry the weight of absence and still find a way forward. We're still learning how to do that—together and apart in our own ways. This exploration has made our garden of marriage so much more lush and beautiful. We cannot be anything to anyone if we are nothing to ourselves. Now more than ever, I feel that with my whole self.

When we were in the thick of all this, I sent texts to my close friends, letting them know that things were feeling heavy for me and my family. I didn't want to just go quiet on them, even though I knew they'd understand if I did. But I was working on not retreating and going ghost without some sort of communication. I shared with them that if I seemed quiet, it's because I needed some space. Their replies were filled with grace, support, and deep compassion.

Okay, sis. I love you. Here if you need me. Send Ryan my love.

Thank you for sharing this with me. I love you and understand. Holding you and the family close to my heart.

I'm grateful that you're taking the space and time you need. I'm always here for you and the fam, know that!

I love this for you, friend. I'll check on you soon—no pressure to respond. I'll be here when you're ready.

Those were just a few of the messages I got back, and they reminded me of how deeply held and supported I am, even in moments when I need to pull away and take care of myself. Collectively, their words helped me recognize that true friendship understands and welcomes the ebb and flow of life, holding space with no strings attached. When we name what we need and want, we make room for people to show up and give us the attention and consideration we deserve.

This type of communication has become the norm for me and the company I keep. Truth be told, I love it here. Having this type of clarity and emotional safety is a godsend. When things feel weighty, or life gets sticky, we honor one another by acknowledging that our communication may change. There's something about that level of transparency that makes the bond feel that much stronger. Open communication can help us all feel more seen, emotionally safe, and included. This is important because open communication fosters understanding and connection, allowing us to be authentic and create spaces for others to do the same. Instead of shutting down, which was my go-to for years, I learned that expressing my feelings creates an opportunity for others to support me. It also deepens trust and builds a sense of belonging. Fostering an environment where we feel valued and emotionally safe helps strengthen the bonds that allow us to feel truly understood and uplifted.

Learning and implementing this can feel daunting, but taking small, intentional steps toward opening up is key. Here are a few things that may help you on your journey:

1. Acknowledge your feelings: Take a moment to reflect on what you're experiencing emotionally. Identifying your feelings can help you express them more clearly.

2. Be honest, but gentle: When you're ready, start by sharing your feelings with someone you trust. You don't need to have all the right words—just be honest. You can say something like, *I've been going through a tough time, and I want to share it with you.*

3. Be clear and set boundaries: Let the person know what you need in that moment—whether it's just to be heard or to receive advice. This can help you set the tone for the support you need or would like to get.

4. Be patient: It takes time to get comfortable with sharing, especially in our tender or painful mo-

ments. Don't rush the process. Start small and with someone that you really trust with your heart and feelings.

Baby steps are still steps. They help ease into more open communication, gradually leading to deeper connections and emotional safety.

Despite the ache that loss and grief left behind, it was important for me to realize how sacred a support system is in times like these. In the fog of grief, the people who understand us—who really know us—can make all the difference. We need people to sit in the trenches with us. To not be scared of the soot and sludge that comes with breaking open. The space we need to fall apart isn't a solitary act—it asks those around us to look at our pain with curiosity and hold out their hands to gather us as we crumble. They don't need to have all the right words or solutions. Our sadness isn't something that needs to be fixed, it's something that must be witnessed—eyes wide and heart open. The more I heal, the more I realize that witnessing is for the brave. The ones who can look deeply and not turn away. The ones who aren't afraid of a little mess being made. Having people in your life whose presence is known *and* felt, even through the quiet storms we endure, shapes and deepens bonds. Ryan and I knew that we had friends who were a phone call away ready to show up and help ease some of the emotional burden. It was even more heartwarming to know that we had people ready to be in the mud with us—no questions asked or burden felt. But even more valuable was having people who understood that sometimes the best support is allowing space—everyone doesn't get it, but the ones who do are irreplaceable.

Reflections

- How does open communication help you feel emotionally safe during times of grief, and how can you invite others to support you through it?

- When navigating grief or heavy emotions, what helps you stay open in your communication instead of shutting down?

- How can you create a space for yourself and others to feel seen and understood when grieving?

- What fears arise when you think about sharing your grief with others, and how can you begin to release those fears to foster a deeper connection?

- How can expressing your grief strengthen the bonds of trust and belonging in your relationships, and how can you communicate your needs more clearly during difficult times?

You are deeply worthy
of the love, support,
and care that we
share with others.
Do not silence yourself
because you don't want
to be too much. You're
allowed to take
up space.

SEVEN

HEALING HIBERNATION

CREATING SPACE FOR INTROSPECTION ALLOWS US TO RE-
turn to ourselves and our relationships with a
rested and clearer mind. Pausing and taking time
to be alone transforms us and our connection. Over the
years, I've learned firsthand how important alone time is.
It's allowed me to better understand myself and my loved
ones. I like to call these times of solitude "healing hibernation." The seasons of walking alone can show you so much
about what and who you truly need in your life. When we
quiet the external noise, we can turn inward without being

distracted away from ourselves, our truth, or our emotions. It's not always easy to step away from the intensity of day-to-day life, but sometimes it's necessary—not as a retreat from the world, but as a return to yourself.

Solitude is a sacred space. The older I get, the more I accept and respect that. It's where we can listen to our thoughts, feel without reacting, and ask ourselves questions that we normally avoid—like, *Why do we believe being small is sometimes where we belong?* Or *Why do we stifle our feelings or grief to avoid taking up too much space?* The answers will come to us slowly, sometimes painfully, if we give ourselves permission to be curious. Even in the discomfort of being alone, clarity can enter. We just have to leave the door open. I am constantly learning that healing isn't just an act of repairing wounds but also a deliberate journey into the layers of the self, welcoming clarity and joy. It's in my moments of alone time that I've discovered parts of me were silenced in and had withered from self-neglect. I used to be so scared of my own company. Terrified about what might creep from under the bed. But something I had to realize along the way is that silence is not the boogeyman. If anything, for me, it's been a hero. Being willing to sit with ourselves without fear that something will emerge and drag us into the darkness we've already escaped from one too many times is a profound act of self-trust. Silence has taught me that the shadows I once feared are often just remnants of old wounds seeking acknowledgment, not threats waiting to consume me. In fact, it's in the stillness that I've found clarity, healing, and the strength to move forward. Rather than running from the quiet, I've learned to embrace it as a space where I can listen to my heart, confront my fears, and emerge more grounded. Silence, when met with openness, becomes an ally—one that helps me reclaim parts of myself that I've been too busy or too afraid to fully notice. Sometimes only in the stillness of solitude can we actively tend to these forgotten pieces of ourselves.

I think it's important to note that my healing hibernation was not about isolation but about creating intentional space to be with myself. I used to seek out good and not-so-good company to avoid the uncomfortable truths that emerged when I was alone. Unlearning this habit was hard. Being avoidant solves nothing—if anything, it creates a deeper disconnect between ourselves and the people we're in relationships with. The presence of others would quiet my clamoring thoughts momentarily, but once they were gone, I was left to confront what I had been avoiding all along. It became clear that I had to learn to face my soft spots with truth instead of shame, fear, or guilt. Over time, I realized that distraction only delays healing. If we constantly fill our lives with external validation, opinions, and advice, our discernment struggles to reach the parts of us that need it most. It wasn't until I allowed myself to sit in silence, without running from it, that I discovered the power of solitude. When we get still, we can find the resilience to face what we have been avoiding, process more clearly, and grow through what we are going through. Even on the days that are challenging to be alone or uncomfortable to get through, silence can transform from something to fear into a place of renewal, where you can reconnect with your inner wisdom and rebuild with authenticity.

All of us have experienced, at some point or other, how loud silence can be. Personally, I filled many of my waking moments with something—work, social events, background noise—to keep myself from being alone with my thoughts. I told myself that being busy meant I was doing well, that if I stayed occupied, I wouldn't have to face the things I'd buried deep down. But eventually, it all caught up with me. Avoiding yourself does not work or serve your greater good.

In 2017, I had a coaching client who was grappling with something similar. During our first sessions, she shared with me that whenever she had a free moment, she'd fill it with something—scrolling through social media, calling a friend, diving into work—anything to avoid being alone with her thoughts. She admitted that she was terrified of what might come up on the pages of her journal if she sat in silence. That fear kept her in a constant state of distraction—so much so that she could no longer pinpoint which thoughts were hers and which weren't.

She came to me with hopes of learning how to face her truth through writing. Working with her was my wake-up call. However, initially I was unsure if I wanted to take her on. Why? Because how could I possibly coach her when I was drowning in my own struggles around stillness? I do not think having a client be my mirror was by coincidence, but it still made me insecure and uneasy.

As she spoke, I saw myself in her words. I realized that I had been doing something similar—running from my own mind, afraid of what stillness might reveal. I stopped my personal writing practice for that very reason. She was looking to me for guidance, but I knew I couldn't lead her anywhere I hadn't been willing to go myself. Working together was a pivotal moment for both of us. As her writing coach, I decided to be honest with her about my struggles, sharing how I had once feared silence, too—and sometimes still do. I told her how uncomfortable it was at first to be vulnerable on the page, but that her quiet moments would become transformative if she allowed them to be. Together, we worked on creating small, intentional moments of stillness in her life, just like I had begun to do for myself.

At first it was small things, like sitting with a morning cup of tea or coffee in silence—no phone, no music, just presence and thoughts. When we started this practice, she said it felt strange at first, as if she were waiting for the ball to drop, but it didn't. Slowly, my client realized the silence wasn't this scary thing she had to fear. It was just space.

Space to think, to feel, to just be. And in that space, she started to hear her voice more clearly—the one she'd been drowning out with all the busyness, which translated to more openness and honesty on the pages of her journal. Watching this client unfold was powerful—she started to find peace in the quiet, confront her fears, and heal. And as she grew, so did I. The writing assignments I'd given her, I was also doing. Working with her taught me the value of walking the talk, doing the inner work alongside my clients, and trusting that sometimes, silence is where the real answers lie.

Eventually, distractions will stop working, and we can't run away from ourselves anymore. When I found myself sitting in silence, it was unsettling. It wasn't just the quiet that made me anxious. What felt most daunting was everything that would surface in it. The unresolved hurt and the

When we get clear, we find freedom.

self-doubt I'd been pushing down for so long were scream-
ing at me. Begging me to come closer and pay attention. It
was in my healing hibernation where I realized how much
of myself I'd been avoiding. How much of my truth I'd
been dismissing. When we choose to stop running from
ourselves, we find ourselves on holy ground. Stillness is
sacred. We become better in our hushed moments, not just
for ourselves but for those we want to share space with.

*A*s time progressed, and my longing for like-minded
community deepened, I learned to cherish the time
where I could sit quietly with my thoughts, where I could
gather clear information from what I wanted and needed.
There was no one to impress or accommodate. No one to
talk me out of or into anything. All I had in those moments
was me—and self-trust was birthed there.

After peeling back the layers and getting to the core
of our truth, maybe what's really terrifying is how much
we will change when we get clear. Our relationships will
shift. Our values will deepen. Our full self can finally surface, and in that will come deep evolution. Change can be
frightening, yes, but it can also be the bridge that brings
you closer to your authentic self. When you reemerge from
your healing hibernation, you will be different. At first, the
changes may feel subtle, and to those around you, they
might not even be noticeable. But within, you'll sense a

transformation taking root. You'll feel the stirrings of new life within—a subtle but profound shift in how you move through the world. Others might still see you through the lens of who you once were, unaware of your internal work, the layers you've shed, and the peace you've reclaimed. Some might expect you to fit back into the same familiar patterns, conversations, and roles. However, what they may not realize is that healing and getting clear isn't just about recovery. It's about renewal. The blessing in taking time to retreat and regroup changes the fabric of our being in ways that can't be undone. Getting quiet so we can get clear teaches us how to soften where we once were stuck in our ways—to pause before reacting and to trust our inner wisdom over the noise of external expectations and distraction. The company you keep will transform for the better—and not necessarily because others have changed but because you have.

I started learning how to show up in my relationships without losing myself. My client shared with me that she started to explore what it looked like to love others without abandoning her needs and how to seek deeper connection to herself and others. She gave an example of her relationship with her sister, who often called her late at night to vent about her problems. In the past, she would stay on the phone for hours, even when she was exhausted or had an early morning ahead, because she didn't want her sister to feel unsupported. But as she began reflecting on what she needed to feel balanced and whole, she realized that staying up late wasn't sustainable. Instead of cutting off the calls entirely, she decided to try a different approach. She told her sister, *"I love you and want to support you, but I can't have late-night conversations anymore. Let's plan a time to talk earlier in the evening when I can be fully present for you."*

Her sister was initially taken aback, but she adapted over time. They started having more meaningful conversations, and my client noticed that she felt less drained and more engaged in their relationship. By naming her capacity out loud, she created space to honor her own needs while still showing up with loving support. It was a powerful reminder that deeper connections don't come from sacrificing ourselves but from bringing our whole selves and truth to the people we cherish.

Gaining enough clarity to recognize when we're losing ourselves is the goal in this work. When we're constantly surrounded by external chatter and input, it can become very easy for us to lose sight of what we actually need from ourselves and within our relationships. One of my greatest realizations on this path has been understanding that solitude acts as a filter, helping me see more clearly who is in alignment with my values, growth, and healing—and who isn't. And sometimes the person out of alignment is me, and me alone.

In my quiet season, I began to recognize the difference

between relationships that uplifted me and those that depleted me. I could feel, without distraction, the energy I received from certain people—the joy, ease, or comfort they brought versus the tension, anxiety, or uncertainty I often ignored. We cannot ignore things away in life and expect to have deep and meaningful relationships. Through solitude, I learned that the company we keep is a direct reflection of the relationship we have with ourselves. When we take the time to nurture our inner world, we naturally gravitate toward those who respect it. We crave deeper connections, grounded in authenticity and mutual respect, rather than surface-level interactions or distractions that only offer temporary comfort. We become more selective, not out of judgment, but out of a deep understanding that not everyone is meant to walk with us for the long haul. The more I embraced my alone time, the more discerning I became about who I invited into my life. I sought relationships where growth was possible, where vulnerability was honored, and where love was expressed through mutual support and consideration. I no longer feared the inner dialogue that solitude encouraged.

When we stop viewing alone time as painful or discouraging, but instead as a vital part of resetting and choosing, the more we start to desire peace, presence, and people who are aligned.

There is something so special about carving out your own healing hibernation, making space for introspection, and reconnecting with yourself. There is a profound power in being by yourself and learning yourself. We don't have to fill our quiet moments with noise and distraction. That will push us away from ourselves and keep us disconnected and unsatisfied. In your hushed moments, may you find the answers you've been seeking and needing all along. Pay attention to yourself and your time. It is only from places of clarity that you will be able to recognize the company that truly deserves to walk alongside you.

Reflections

- Think about a time when solitude brought you clarity about yourself or your relationships. What did you learn about your needs, desires, or boundaries? How did that experience shape your current relationships?

- What does "healing hibernation" mean to you? How can you create more intentional alone time to focus on your growth and self-discovery?

- Think about the relationships in your life right now. Which ones feel nurturing and aligned with your values, and which feel draining or misaligned? What steps can you take to cultivate more intentional connections with those who uplift you?

- How do you feel when you spend time alone? Is it comfortable, peaceful, or perhaps uncomfortable or unsettling? How can you deepen your relationship with yourself to make alone time feel sacred and restorative?

- When you think about your ideal community or circle, who comes to mind, and why? How does their presence align with the insights you've gained from your alone time?

Being by yourself for a season is sacred. The peace you find cannot be replicated in the company of others.

EIGHT

THE QUIET STRENGTH OF LETTING GO

*Y*OU CAN'T ALWAYS BE THERE FOR PEOPLE WHO AREN'T ready or willing to receive you. Like the friend who keeps conversations light, steering away from vulnerability because it feels safer for them. Or the relative who says, *"I'm fine,"* even when their energy says otherwise, unsure how to let someone in. Or the partner who avoids deep conversations with humor or dismissal, not because they don't care but because they may not know how to navigate those uncomfortable waters. These moments aren't about your lack of care or effort—they reflect where others might be in their own journey. Everything isn't personal, and sometimes the most compassionate thing you can do is honor their pace, meet them where they are, and allow them the space to lower their walls when they're ready. Connection thrives when built on mutual readiness, and trusting that timing is an act of love. It doesn't matter how much you care or how deeply you want to help—you cannot force a connection with someone who keeps you at a distance. And yet, acknowledging this limitation doesn't make it any easier. Letting go of the desire to fix, heal, or hold someone close when they're pushing you away is one of the hardest lessons to learn. But with it comes this nugget of clarity: Our love and support can only go as far as the other person allows. It's natural to want to be there for the people you care about—in friendship, love, and family, we instinctively want to give and show up. We want to be the safe harbor in a storm, the shoulder to lean on, the one who provides comfort. Yet, there's a delicate balance between showing up for someone and recognizing when to step back. Sometimes the most compassionate act isn't giving more but allowing space. We can try to be a supportive friend, intentional partner, and caring family member—but if the other person doesn't have the capacity or readiness to receive that care, our efforts will fall flat. Or worse, create an even deeper wedge of disconnection.

The hardest part is accepting that their season of life may require distance. They may need time, space, or even a detour through struggle to find their way. And as much as we want to help, their journey is not ours to steer.

A few years ago, one of my close friends—let's call him Christian—and I approached a fork in the road of our relationship. He was going through a really tough time with his girlfriend, and I was on the outside looking in. He'd ask me for advice often—and, of course, I wanted to be a safe place for him to land. However, whenever it was time to have hard conversations about what he was dealing with, I was met with defensiveness every single time. I could tell that the turmoil in his relationship was causing a major overwhelm in his life. As his friend, I was on the receiving end of those same feelings of overwhelm. I was stressed and frustrated with him. Watching him suffer was maddening to witness, in part because he and his girlfriend were constantly at odds but also because it was draining for *me* to have the air sucked out of the room with his dysfunction. The consistent back and forth, the fighting, and everything else in between often left me caught in the middle. I knew he was in a tender space, and even though it was gut-wrenching to see, he didn't *really* want my help or feedback like he said he did. The times I tried to be there, he shut me out. There wasn't much that I could say that wouldn't cause his walls to go up. I could tell that he was torn between wanting me to mind my own business and desperately wanting my input. It was a weird place to be in our friendship.

As his friend, watching him consistently be in distress was troubling. To me, it was clear what should happen: *Leave her!* He was with someone who treated him awful. She lied to him at every turn, gaslit and manipulated him, cheated on him, and enjoyed causing rifts in all of his relationships. The drama was endless, and it was a mess to observe. But in spite of how clear it was to me that he should walk away, it did not matter because it wasn't my decision to make.

We've all been there at some point or another: We've watched our friends or loved ones making choices we wouldn't, ignoring what we think is the best path to take. Watching them go through emotional chaos is painful and frustrating. We can often feel helpless and, at times, even angry. Because their life isn't ours, we may not ever be able to understand why people stay in unhealthy situations or tolerate harmful and toxic behavior. Observing Christian's relationship, every part of me wanted to intervene, to shake him awake, and help him see the truth. But no matter how much I wanted to solve this problem for him, I had to remind myself that it wasn't my decision to make. His journey was his own, and I had to accept that. Through this experience, I became familiar with the fact that sometimes the most compassionate thing we can do for the people we love is to let them navigate their own storms. Even with the best intentions, we can't save someone from their own choices. And sometimes our attempts to help, to fix, only push them further away—and that was the last thing I wanted. I had to learn to honor the distance and accept that my friend had the autonomy to choose his path, even if it wasn't the one I thought was best for him.

Here's the real issue with what was happening: Every time I was with Christian, I felt completely off balance. My spirit was unsettled. My heart was broken, and my energy was drained. I'd come home tense, frustrated, and unable to let it go, venting to my husband and staying stuck in Christian's cycle of chaos for what felt like days. My mind would replay the conversations, and the heaviness of dysfunction that wasn't even mine to carry seemed to follow me. And while that is true, Christian and his girlfriend's relationship struggles weren't just theirs anymore—they were starting to seep into my own emotional space, creating a ripple effect of pain and overwhelm. It was like I was carrying a piece of their chaos with me, and it became clear that this wasn't sustainable. Something had to change, because while I cared deeply, I realized I couldn't keep sacrificing my peace.

It's easy to blur the lines between support and control in friendships, especially the close ones. We think that because we love someone, we should have a say in their choices, but love doesn't work that way. Respecting someone's autonomy means trusting that they can figure things out for themselves, even if the process is gut-wrenching and unbearable to see in action. The pattern that my friend was caught in was exhausting to witness. Eventually, I made the necessary decision to take a step back. It pained me to do so, but I had to set a boundary. With compassion and gentleness in hand, I called my friend and told him that while I loved and cared for him deeply, I couldn't continue to be his sounding board for this toxic relationship. My voice trembled as I explained that it was taking a toll on my emotional well-being and that I needed to protect my peace. As a final act of care and support, I gave him a list of therapists to reach out to for support. I desperately wanted him to be okay. And while this was a hard conversation to have because I didn't want him to feel abandoned, I realized that I had to prioritize my mental health.

A knot of tears caught in my throat as we spoke. I reassured him that I would be there when he got to the other side of this, but I couldn't continue to engage in conversations that left me feeling drained and frustrated. Setting that boundary wasn't easy—a part of me feared he'd take it the wrong way or create even more distance between us. But I knew that if our friendship was to survive, it had to be built on mutual respect, including respect for each other's limits.

It took me quite some time to trust that in setting the boundary, we would be stronger in the long run. I wasn't abandoning my friend, but there were days when it felt like I was. Choosing to protect ourselves from being consumed by situations that (1) we have no control over and (2) have nothing to do with us is an act of self-preservation—even when it comes to people that we adore and value. Boundaries are sacred. They can make space for our friendships to evolve in healthier ways where we can offer support without sacrificing our sanity. No longer inserting myself did create distance between us. It wasn't comfortable, and there were moments when I felt like I needed to be there at his beck and call. But I realized that true friendship isn't about control but trust. Trusting that, in time, he would find his way. Trusting that even in the midst of his pain, he was doing the best he could. And trusting that our friendship could survive this space in between even if it didn't look the way it once did.

All of this can feel like a lot to move through and think about, especially when we are trying to be a vessel for care, community, and comfort. Here are some things that helped me:

Practice loving detachment: Detachment doesn't mean you stop caring for people. It means you lovingly release the need to fix what isn't yours to repair. You can continue being loving and supportive while also acknowledging that their journey is theirs and yours is yours. Putting down baggage that is not yours to carry is essential for creating more mindful connections. This approach may not be easy at first, but with practice it allows us to remain compassionate without depleting ourselves emotionally.

Set healthy boundaries: Establishing clear emotional boundaries for yourself is necessary. Clear boundaries help us learn to recognize when our attempts to help are causing more harm than good. They also create space for us to look at things more objectively. In the course of navigating and learning loving detachment, we may have to release control and give ourselves permission to take a step back when needed. This practice welcomes more self-compassion by allowing us to protect our emotional well-being while honoring the other person's space.

Practice patience with the process: Patience is key—with our loved ones and with ourselves. Acknowledging and understanding that personal growth and healing take time. We all have our own journeys to walk. No one's path to clarity, connection, and compassion is linear. Being intentional about practicing patience gives yourself and others space and grace to navigate life's ebbs and flows at their own pace. As challenging as it may feel, patience fosters compassion and trust, as you release the need for immediate change or resolution.

Reframe your expectations: Managing your expectations may look like learning to (respectfully) mind your business. Instead of focusing on how the other person should respond or change, shift your attention to what you can control. The only things in your hands are your actions and responses. Remind yourself that offering love and support doesn't guarantee a specific outcome, and that's okay. Creating a heart of compassion means accepting things as they are, not as we wish them to be.

*H*onoring the distance doesn't mean giving up on someone. It means respecting their need to grow, even if that growth takes them in a different direction than we'd hoped. Letting go of the need to regulate someone else's journey is an act of love, not abandonment. It's an acknowledgment that we can love folks but can't walk their path for them. Letting go creates space for a deeper, more honest connection with a foundation of mutual compassion and understanding. To my surprise, my friend embraced the boundary. He acknowledged that he hadn't been showing up as his best self and admitted that he'd started trauma-dumping on the people who cared about him. I was taken aback by his honesty. He then shared that he felt overwhelmed and had plans of breaking things off with his girlfriend, but needed time to reflect and make decisions without seeking approval or validation from others. Listening to this, I felt a wave of relief wash over me. I was incredibly proud of him. I also heard him say that he didn't need me in the capacity that I assumed he did. We ended our conversation by exchanging *I love you*s, and I assured him I'd be here whenever he was ready to reconnect. The heaviness on both of us had been lifted. We understood that we needed space to regroup and find clarity in order for our friendship to be healthy, helpful, and aligned.

As tricky as this situation was, it became even more clear that allowing others to walk their path, even if it's without us, is loving. Watching someone we care about remain stuck in patterns that don't serve them can feel excruciating, especially when we know they deserve so much more. We want to fix what's broken, guide them to better choices, or be their refuge—but their healing is not our responsibility. Their path is their own. Learning to honor this is necessary.

Letting go in this way requires a kind of compassion

that is both deep and quiet. It's a recognition that we can love someone without carrying their burdens. We can care without overstepping boundaries. There is immense power in accepting that we can't save someone from their choices, dysfunctions, or inner chaos. What we can do is offer love from a distance, respecting their process while still honoring our truth. Instances like this are also a call to be compassionate; releasing the urge to intervene isn't a failure of love—it's an act of faith. We have to have faith in the people we care about. We've all had seasons of feeling lost before, and no one, no matter how much they love us, could fix that for us. Thoughtfully and compassionately stepping back doesn't mean we're failing or letting people down. Even in the doubt that may emerge or the discomfort that creeps in, all of this is an opportunity to practice deeper acceptance and intentional loving-kindness.

Reflections:

- What does it look like to love someone from a distance while still honoring your boundaries and truth? How can you practice both compassion and self-respect in this process?

- Reflect on when you felt the urge to intervene in someone else's journey. What emotions came up for you? How did stepping back challenge your idea of what it means to love and support someone?

- How can you cultivate deeper faith in the people you care about?

- What discomfort or doubt arises when you step back from someone you love who is struggling? How can you reframe those feelings as opportunities to practice acceptance without fixing or changing the situation?

- How have your own seasons of feeling lost shaped your understanding of what it means to be supported?

You deserve to
be in spaces and
relationships that
make you happy—
that feed your soul
and help you grow.

NINE

THE DUALITY OF LOSS AND GRATITUDE

*O*VER THE YEARS, I'VE COME TO UNDERSTAND THAT when a relationship ends, it doesn't erase the beauty of what was shared. The love, laughter, and moments of tenderness remain woven into your life's fabric. It's human to miss people when they're no longer in our lives, to feel the ache of their absence, and to hold on to the memories that brought you joy. These memories don't lose their value simply because the relationship has run its course. I've come to make peace with that.

I've also learned that holding on to every relationship isn't required for a full or loving life. We're often taught to forgive at all costs, to smooth over fractures, and to ignore how we've been hurt in the name of keeping the peace—in the vein of blood is thicker than water, or *but you've known them for so long*. We're told to stay, to bend, to compromise ourselves for the sake of others' comfort or potential, even when doing so diminishes our light. Choosing to unlearn this is an act of self-preservation. I've come to understand that choosing not to repair a relationship isn't an act of cruelty. It's an act of care—care for yourself, your boundaries, your mental and emotional health.

The deeper I journey into my own healing, the more I come to realize that reconciliation is not a requirement, particularly when the relationship in question drains more than it restores, and harms more than it heals. While I hold space for the possibility of repair in certain circumstances, I've also learned that there are times when forgiveness must be an inward act—a quiet, personal reckoning that doesn't need the hand-holding of reconnection. Every relationship isn't meant to be mended, and not every ending comes with the closure we crave. It took me years to make peace with this. There are moments when we must accept that closeness with certain people isn't possible or healthy, no matter how much we might wish it otherwise. Letting go often means finding the courage to release our disappointment and grief, choosing not to invite someone back into our lives, even if we still carry a longing for what could have been. This process—grieving without reopening the door—can be both the hardest and most liberating step toward true peace.

In the spring of 2024, I came to a pivotal realization: It was time to end a five-year friendship with someone I'd long suspected didn't truly like me. For the sake of this story, let's call her Nikki. It wasn't just that she didn't seem to like me—it became evident through her behavior and actions that she didn't want me in her life. There was no dramatic falling-out or overt conflict, but an undeniable sense of unease always lingered whenever we were together. Our friendship felt perpetually awkward, as though the energy between us was misaligned and constantly unsteady. Like clockwork, the atmosphere would shift whenever we got together. I found myself walking on eggshells, unsure why there was tension. Our being friends wasn't easy. It was challenging, uncertain, and, if I'm being honest, it was weird. It didn't start this way, though. In the beginning, our connection felt natural and comfortable. Somewhere along the line, though, things changed—subtly, yet significantly. I can't pinpoint exactly when or why, but the shift was impossible to ignore.

One instance stands out very clearly for me. We had plans to meet for brunch at a cute spot we'd visited a few times before. A couple of other friends were joining us, and I was running late. I remember the growing anxiety building in my chest as I realized I wouldn't make it on time. I'd been having a rough morning but didn't think rescheduling would be well received. Nikki's voice echoed in my mind— her passive-aggressive comments in the past whenever I was late or not quick enough to respond to her texts and calls were always coated in sarcastic laughter that stuck with me. Hearing her say things like, *"I'm not inviting you because you'll be late,"* or, *"I don't call you because you never answer my calls,"* lingered in my mind longer than I'd like to admit. Those words weren't just casual remarks—they carried the weight of her disappointment, reflecting how my actions, or lack thereof, had been interpreted. I valued her time, energy, and presence deeply, and the thought of Nikki feeling unimportant to me stung in ways I couldn't ignore. After those hints were dropped, I knew I had to do better. I made it a priority to show up for her in the ways that mattered. I started arriving on time, even early. When she called, I answered or made sure to call her back as soon as possible. It wasn't just about proving something to her—it was about doing my best to honor the friendship and ensure she knew she was an important person in my life.

But that day, no matter how much I had tried to adjust and show her I cared, I wasn't going to make it on time. And I knew it might undo some of the progress I'd worked so hard to rebuild. The frustration with myself was sharp, but so was the awareness of how much this would likely matter to her.

My heart felt like it had sunk into my stomach as I texted the group apologizing, letting them know I was running behind. *"Y'all I'm so sorry. I got caught up with the kids, had to stop for gas, and missed my exit. Forgive me. This morning isn't going as planned at all,"* I explained. The others responded graciously: *"No problem! We're moving slow. Take your time. It's all good, sis."* Their understanding brought a small wave of relief. But Nikki? She said nothing. When I finally arrived, I spotted them at the table and hurried over. Nikki barely looked at me, her face a mask of indifference. *Damn it, she's pissed*—I thought to myself. Her eyes didn't meet mine as I offered a sheepish smile, and the only acknowledgment she gave was a brief, tight-lipped nod that felt more like a dismissal than a greeting. I sat down, my heart heavy with the unmistakable weight of her upset. The others were warm and welcoming, but Nikki's silence spoke louder than any words. At that moment, I knew—this would be the last time we gathered like this. The weeks prior had been weird with her. I thought maybe she was going through something. I'd asked a few times but was met with her usual, *"I'm fine, girl."* The realization that our friendship was likely going to wither settled over me with surprising clarity and a strange sense of comfort. I didn't need or want to keep fighting for a connection that had already unraveled.

After that brunch date, I asked her for the fourth time in the five years we'd known each other: *"Do you like me? Did I do something? Before brunch things were off and now things are really off, what is going on?"* Asking the same questions in different ways had become exhausting. She was the only person in my life that I had these issues with. I was tired of dealing with the consistent off feelings and asking if and why things with us had changed. Walking on eggshells was uncomfortable, annoying, and hurtful. Tiptoeing in our relationships with people is unhealthy and disruptive to our nervous system and peace of mind. At one point, I felt like I was going crazy. I remember asking my husband, *"WHAT am I doing wrong here?"* Nikki's responses to my questions were vague, nonchalant, and unclear. She would say a lot by not really saying anything at all—leaving me questioning myself and wondering if I was overthinking, being too sensitive, or simply making things up. I'd find myself questioning if it was just me. Or perhaps I really was just an inadequate or inconsiderate friend. I think that's why I stayed so long. I thought I was the problem, and I wanted to fix it. I wanted to prove to her that I was good and worthy of her friendship. My thoughts were always swirling, chasing each other like cat and mouse. I was trying my best to find ways not to be on her bad side. By the end of our friendship, the whole situation got more and more strange. I didn't like it and decided I was no longer going to put up with it to keep the peace or be in her good graces.

Early on in our friendship she showed up differently—welcoming, warm, reciprocal, and open. I remember us meeting each other in understanding and flexibility. However, I noticed, the closer we tried to get, the more she started putting up walls. I'd caught glimpses of her softer side when she needed to "pick my brain" about business or vent about life, but those moments didn't last. One minute, she was present and engaged, and the next, distant and withdrawn. Nikki was often hot-and-cold, which left me confused and second-guessing everything—including myself. It was like trying to build a bridge while the other side kept crumbling—it just didn't feel sustainable. I think we both tried our best to create sisterhood, but we just could not get it to stick. Nikki would constantly make remarks about my being "famous" and not wanting to "bother me," which felt odd. To me, neither of these things were true. People knew me but I'm not famous, and not once did I feel like she was a burden. I welcomed all of her, or at least I thought I did. In hindsight, something felt off from the beginning, but I ignored the signs. I realize now that the foundation of any relationship must be built on shared truths and mutual understanding. The cracks in ours were subtle at first—a stray comment here, an uneasy laugh there—but it was all telling.

Many of us ignore the signs we see because, rightfully so, we want our relationships to work. We want to believe that effort alone can be the glue. That it can mend the gaps and offer us what we need to walk through life together. But effort alone is not enough. Relationships require more than trying, they need doing, too. The lesson I learned from this is to honor the unspoken feelings that arise, even when it's uncomfortable. Asking for clarity in your relationships is not a bother or a burden. To the right people, it's a love language—an invitation to be vulnerable, honest, and compassionate. When something feels off, it's not a call to judge or fix—it's a call to listen, explore, and sometimes accept what the truth really is: Every connection won't evolve into the sacred bond we hope for. This doesn't mean either person failed—it simply means we met, we tried, and we taught each other something about what we need, what we'll accept, and how we'll show up in the future.

Friend breakups are never easy, and a lot of the time they sneak up on us after sweeping things under the rug or letting certain behaviors slide that normally wouldn't. Deciding to step away from relationships that are not healthy or in alignment isn't a failure. It's an act of self-preservation and self-respect. The end of a relationship brings a lot of emotions to the surface. Sadness, anger, relief, nostalgia—it all comes to a head when something we love starts to dissolve. It's natural to grieve what is no longer, to feel the weight of unmet expectations and lost potential. Grieving a relationship doesn't only mean mourning the person—it's also the realization that you're grieving the future you imagined with them. It's a tender process but can also lead to healing and clarity.

I second-guessed myself after I decided to end things with Nikki. I replayed our last encounter repeatedly, wondering if I could have handled it differently. There were moments when I asked myself if I was being too sensitive or too quick to give up. But the truth was, I had already spent years trying to make it work—asking questions like, *What am I doing wrong? How can I fix this?*—when, deep down, I knew the weight of the friendship wasn't mine to carry alone.

I decided not having another conversation with her was in my best interest. We clearly were not on the same page, and I didn't have another "can we talk" conversation in me. Backing away was a gradual process at first. I stopped initiating calls and texts, something I had always done to keep the connection alive. She also never reached out. I stopped trying to fix things, stopped asking how I could make things better, and instead focused on protecting my heart.

After the friendship ended, a tender and difficult moment for me was seeing Nikki repeatedly appear in my friends' comment sections on social media. It's hard to put into words, but it felt intentional, like she was trying to provoke or manipulate by engaging in ways that were out of character for her. After a few months of sitting with this discomfort, I decided to block her if I saw her name again—something that I rarely feel the need to do. I knew it was a definitive and necessary step. Protecting my peace online is just as important as protecting it in my everyday life, and I realized I had to take that step for my well-being.

The final decision to cut ties completely wasn't easy. I cried about it, journaled about it, and talked it through with my husband more times than I can count. But I knew that staying in the friendship was costing me too much—my energy, my clarity, and my sense of self. I realized that no matter how much I cared for Nikki, I couldn't keep pouring into a relationship that left me feeling unsure and not enough. Letting go wasn't about anger or resentment—it was about acceptance. I had to accept that I couldn't change the dynamic on my own, that Nikki wasn't in a place to meet me in the middle. It wasn't a dramatic breakup or a heated argument—it was a quiet, deliberate choice to release something that no longer felt healthy, comforting, or kind.

There's definitely a bittersweetness to walking away from someone you once held so dear, but there's also relief. Relief in knowing you honored yourself by choosing ease. And while the doubts and second-guessing lingered for a while, I eventually realized that this decision, as hard as it was, was a necessary act of self-respect.

For a time, the memories of our good times would float to the surface. I replayed laughter and conversations that once felt light and joyful, and I almost let those glimpses of goodness convince me to reopen the door. A key lesson for me was understanding that reflecting on the good times does not mean I have to reenter the relationship. It's possible to honor what once was, to smile at the memories, to appreciate the lessons the connection offered—and still move forward without looking back. Nostalgia isn't a summons. It's a reminder of a chapter in your life. It's okay to remember while (also) staying committed to your decision to let go.

Liberation, I've learned, isn't always loud or dramatic. Sometimes it's a quiet yet clear decision to choose yourself. To trust that letting go doesn't erase the joy you once shared but instead makes room for relationships rooted in mutual respect, care, and love. Letting go can be a form of gratitude, not just for the lessons learned but for the courage to move beyond what no longer aligns. Releasing a relationship doesn't mean forgetting, and it doesn't mean bitterness or hatred. I wish Nikki the best and I am glad our friendship is over. The emotional games and chaos were too much. We couldn't meet each other in friendship, and that is okay. Gratitude and grief can coexist. You can feel thankful for what the relationship taught you—about love, boundaries, and yourself—while recognizing that its ending was necessary. Some relationships serve a purpose, but not every relationship is meant to be enduring. Seasons change. People grow together and apart. There are lessons and blessings in both.

Reflections

- **Your Feelings Are Sacred:** Reflect on someone you miss deeply. How can you honor those feelings without judgment?

- **Love Exists Beyond Distance:** Write about a broken relationship you chose not to mend. How can you hold space for the love that once was, while honoring your decision to protect your peace?

- **Healing Through Gratitude:** Think about a joyful memory or lesson from a past relationship. How can gratitude for that experience help you move toward closure and healing?

- **Trust Your Inner Wisdom:** Recall a moment when you prioritized your mental health over maintaining a connection. What did that decision teach you about your self-worth?

- **Permission to Move Forward:** Imagine yourself writing a new chapter in your life story. What does releasing the past and embracing hope look like for you today?

You have the right to release relationships entirely, especially ones that are harmful to your mental health and emotional well-being. Memories can be cherished without anchoring you to the past.

TEN

THE GIVER

THIS YEAR, I'VE BEEN SITTING WITH A TENDER TRUTH: I am often the giver who pours and shows up with care and intention. I'm the friend who initiates, who plans the monthly meet-ups, who invites others for a walk or a cup of tea. I'm the one constantly thinking of ways to nurture the connections I treasure. But lately, I've noticed how rarely that same energy is reflected back to me. It's not that I expect grand gestures or constant attention, but I long to be considered, to feel held in someone's heart with the same tenderness I extend to others. Admitting this has been a struggle. I've worried that voicing these feelings might come across as needy, ungrateful, or worse—

whiny. But clarity often emerges from discomfort, so I've let myself sit with these emotions. What I've uncovered feels both like a revelation and an old wound: the ache of feeling like an afterthought. It's not easy to hold, but I'm learning to honor it without dismissing or rationalizing it away. Yes, people are busy. Yes, life is full. But I am busy, too. Life is full for me, too. And still, I make space.

Relationships are vital to me—not because I feel obligated, but because they anchor me. They remind me of who I am beyond the roles of mother, wife, and author. They ground me. And I've realized that while I'm deeply honored to pour into the people I love, I've been quietly craving that same intention in return. Throughout the years, I've had to confront this truth: Not everyone sees relationships the way I do. For me, they are a source of grounding and growth, but for others, they may not hold the same weight. This doesn't make anyone wrong or lessen my love for them. But it stings. It's human to feel the ache of unmet expectations. Yet as I reflect, I'm reminded that grace is essential—for myself and others. People's priorities are different, and their capacity for connection fluctuates. This isn't a failure of love; it simply reflects life's complexity.

One morning, when I was in the thick of these feelings, I sat down to meditate. As I sat against the wall, back straight, breaths deep, I let the truth of my feelings settle into my spirit. I held myself with compassion, saying to myself: *It's okay that people don't show up in the same ways I do.* It's okay that their priorities and emotional landscapes differ from mine. That doesn't mean my feelings of sadness or longing are invalid. Both can coexist: acceptance of what is, addressing what's feeling true, and adjusting how I show up or not. Acceptance starts with giving yourself permission to feel what you're feeling without judgment or shame. For me, that looked like journaling about my emotions after meditation instead of pushing them away. I wrote down the disappointment I felt, the longing for reciprocity, and the exhaustion that came from constantly being the initiator. Seeing my feelings on the page helped me recognize their validity and reminded me that they are not a sign of weakness—they are part of my humanity. Addressing these emotions meant getting curious about them. I asked myself questions like: *What patterns have brought me here? Am I giving in ways that feel aligned with my capacity? Have I communicated my needs clearly?* I also started having gentle, honest conversations with those closest to me. For instance, I told a friend how much her thoughtfulness meant to me and shared how it felt when I noticed it was missing. These moments of vulnerability were hard but necessary—and to my surprise, they were met with kindness and understanding. Adjusting required me to reflect on how I could realign my energy in relationships. I began setting boundaries around how much I was giving, choosing to invest more deeply in friendships that felt nourishing and reciprocal. This didn't mean cutting people off but, instead, shifting my expectations and re-allocating my energy. I also gave myself permission to step back when I felt stretched too thin. For example, instead of initiating plans every month, I paused and waited to see who would reach out. That space gave me clarity about which relationships felt mutual and which ones I was carrying alone. These three steps—accepting, addressing, and adjusting—are not linear. They require ongoing practice and empathy. But through this process, I've discovered that honoring my needs doesn't just deepen my relationships with others—it deepens my relationship with myself. By giving myself what I need, I've started to feel more whole, less resentful, and more at peace with the ebbs and flows of connection.

The older I get, the more I understand that relationships require harmony, effort, and action. Connection cannot thrive in passivity. And while I deeply value showing up for others, I'm learning to balance that with showing up for myself. It's not selfish to want reciprocity—it's human. It's not wrong to crave relationships where energy flows both ways, leaving both people feeling seen, cared for, and replenished. Something I reflect on now more than ever is the roles we occupy in our relationships and how unspoken dynamics can quietly define them. For years, I've been seen as "the strong one"—the one who has it all together, who doesn't need help, who will figure it out—the one who is too busy, too fulfilled, or too self-sufficient to rely on anyone. These assumptions, though often unintentional, have left me feeling deeply unseen at times. The pang doesn't just stem from being overlooked—it comes from the absence of curiosity and intention, the sense that no one is asking, *What might she need? How might I lighten her load?*

What I've realized is that to be cared for, we must first be considered. Care doesn't appear in a vacuum—it requires someone to pause, reflect, and ask themselves how they can show up for you. And yet, I've also come to see that if we're always performing strength or independence, rarely expressing vulnerability or articulating our needs, we unintentionally reinforce these dynamics. We become the friend who is "fine," the person others assume doesn't need checking in on, the one who will always handle things solo. I wore the "strong one" label like a badge of honor for years. But I've since learned that unshakable strength often comes at the expense of being human. By not wanting people to see me struggle, I denied them—and myself—opportunities for a deeper connection. I carried so much silently, thinking it was my responsibility alone. Over time, I realized the weight of those unspoken roles and how damaging they could be to me and the relationships I wanted to nurture.

Something to remember when navigating these emotional spaces is that strength doesn't mean shouldering everything alone. It means allowing others to share the load when you need it. To shift these unspoken dynamics, I had to start being honest with the people in my life. I started small, letting loved ones know when I was overwhelmed or tired. I practiced asking for help, even when I thought doing it alone would be easier. I began expressing deeper gratitude when someone remembered me or checked in, reinforcing how much it meant and how much I needed it. These small steps chipped away at the false narrative of invulnerability I had built and created space for more reciprocity. People don't know what we don't tell them. I've also learned the power of naming and reexamining these dynamics within myself. When I sense that someone has cast me into the "strong one" role, I gently challenge it. I might say something like, "I know I seem like I have it all together sometimes, but I don't, and I could use some support right now." Or "I love being the one who shows up for others, but it would mean a lot to have someone check on me, too." These moments of truth-telling have been uncomfortably liberating. They've shown me that relationships have the space to grow richer and more balanced when we allow ourselves to be seen fully—not just in strength but in tenderness. To be considered, we must make ourselves known. The people in our lives are not mind readers, even if we wish they were. That's the lesson I've been sitting with: I am worthy of curiosity, intention, and care, and it starts with me giving others permission to step into those roles. It's a gentle recalibration of connection—one that I'm learning, again and again, to embrace.

I talked with my friend Fina about these feelings a few years ago, and she brought something important to light. She shared, "I take care of everyone, but who takes care of me? You're one of the only people who checks in on me." Her words echoed a question I've carried quietly: *Who is pouring into me?* I thought back to when I had been navigating a particularly hard season—balancing work deadlines, family responsibilities, and my mounting exhaustion. I'd been so overwhelmed that even asking for help felt like too much. One day, this same friend texted me out of the blue: *"I'm thinking about you. How can I support you right now?"*

That message stopped me in my tracks. It wasn't elaborate or grand, but it was intentional, and it reminded me of how deeply a small act of care can resonate. Fina didn't assume I was fine just because I hadn't said otherwise. That's something I love about her. Instead, she was curious, thoughtful, and present. In that moment, I felt seen, which gave me the courage to say, *"I'm struggling. I don't even know what I need, but thank you for asking."* Her willingness to check in created space for me to be vulnerable without feeling like a burden. It's a simple moment I've carried with me—a reminder of how intentionality can soften even the hardest days.

I've had to make peace with this truth: voicing my need to be cared for does not diminish the joy I find in giving. It's taken me time to fully embrace that my longing to feel emotionally held is not a betrayal of my generosity. Both can exist together—giving with an open heart and quietly wishing for the same care in return.

Thoughtfulness holds deep meaning. To be remembered, checked on, and cared for in small yet intentional ways—these gestures breathe life into relationships. Friendship has taught me that (1) thoughtfulness looks and feels different to everyone; and (2) thoughtful moments don't always just happen on their own. They require us to name our needs and create space for honest and vulnerable dialogue. Relationships flourish not through assumption or habit but through curiosity, intention, and a shared willingness to show up for one another. I continue

Pay attention to who shows up when you need them the most.

to sit with these truths as relationships change and evolve and trace their roots. Even today, I'm learning to let go of patterns that no longer serve me—patterns of over-giving, overextending, and accepting less than what I deserve in return. It's not that I want to stop being thoughtful—I simply want to feel the safety and joy of knowing that the care I extend is reciprocated. We all do.

Being in a relationship with others is truly a practice of vulnerability, grace, and honesty. Naming my needs feels uncomfortable and tender, but it is also liberating. It's a way of reclaiming my worth and saying to myself, *You deserve the same love and care you give others.* This unlearning and naming is a gift I'm giving myself. It has allowed me to build deeper connections with the people who value me and want to show up for me in meaningful ways. For example, when I told Fina that I'd been feeling unseen, she responded with such tenderness. She started making small but intentional gestures—sending a text to check in, leaving a voice note when she knew I had a big day ahead, or scheduling deliberate time for us to connect over FaceTime. Those moments have reminded me of the beauty in being cared for, not because I had to demand it but because I had the courage to share my truth. It's also shifted how I move through my relationships. By naming my needs, I've created more balance in my connections. When I used to take on everything—planning, coordinating, and holding space for everyone—I often felt depleted.

But now, I've started asking for help or collaboration, like inviting friends to co-plan gatherings or take turns initiating check-ins. This small shift has lightened my load and deepened my relationships. It's shown me that reciprocity is not just about receiving but about creating space for others to show up, too. Most important, naming my needs has brought me closer to myself. It's given me permission to acknowledge when I feel unseen or unappreciated without shame. It's a gentle reminder that honoring my own worth is not selfish but necessary—and in doing so, I'm modeling for others that it's okay to ask for the love and care we all deserve.

Walking through the ebbs and flows of friendship, I am reminded that relationships flourish in intentional reciprocity, compassionate communication, and radical clarity. That connection is strongest when it is tended to with mutual care. And so—I am choosing to honor both the love I give and the love I am worthy of receiving. In doing so, I hope to find a deeper sense of balance—one where my heart remains generous, but my well doesn't run dry. Asking for what we need is not a weakness. It is not selfish to seek relationships that replenish rather than deplete. It is, perhaps, the most profound act of self-love.

Reflections

- What does reciprocity look like for you in your relationships? Reflect on how mutual care has shown up in your connections and where there might be imbalances.

- In what ways do you communicate your needs to others? Consider whether there are opportunities to practice more clarity or vulnerability when expressing what you need.

- What relationships in your life feel replenishing, and which ones feel depleting? Identify the relationships that pour into you and those needing recalibration or more clarity.

- How do you tend to your well-being while showing up for others? Reflect on whether your generosity leaves space for your care and how you might create more harmony in your friendships.

- What fears or hesitations arise when you think about asking for what you need? Explore the stories or thoughts that may hold you back from pursuing the love and support you deserve.

ELEVEN

ACKNOWLEDGE, ACCEPT, ADJUST

*T*HE RELATIONSHIPS WE'RE A PART OF ARE MIRRORS. They reflect the cadence of our lives. At times, they're unpredictable, layered, and complex. Sharing our lives with others isn't straightforward. To love and be loved is to open ourselves up to vulnerability and be truthful about what we are willing and unwilling to accept in our connections with others. As I sit with all of this in my life, I've returned to three guiding principles: **acknowledge, accept, and adjust**. These haven't just been abstract ideas for me. They've become practices—a way to nurture gratitude, foster clarity, and settle into my inner peace.

A few years ago, I experienced a moment of reckoning in a friendship that had been a significant part of my life for nearly fifteen years. Eva and I walked through a lot together, both the good and the challenging, and our connection felt like one of those lifelong bonds that could weather anything. But as time passed, I noticed a tension building beneath the surface that I could no longer ignore. I realized I was carrying a silent but growing resentment. Embedded deep in my heart was a tenderness that was hard to describe. I felt that I was the only one putting effort into keeping our connection alive. I initiated plans, checked in, and ensured the relationship stayed intact, while it felt like Eva had grown comfortable with letting me carry the weight of it all. The frustration had been simmering for months, but I hadn't allowed myself to fully name it. I harbored some shame and guilt for having these thoughts about her. In a sense, they felt wrong—not in an overtly negative way, but in the subtle ways that only show up when you pause long enough to listen to your gut. It was the kind of wrong that leaves you questioning your own perceptions, wondering if you're asking too much or overanalyzing things. I'd walk away from conversations feeling a little emptier, a little more unseen. It wasn't anything Eva said directly, though, which is what confused me. It was more about what she didn't say, the effort she didn't put in. I started to feel like I was carrying the weight of our sisterhood by myself, and with each unreciprocated text or last-minute cancelled time to connect, the weight felt like too much to hold alone. I dreaded bringing this to her attention. Eva wasn't the easiest friend to talk to when approached with something like this. I also didn't want to make her feel blamed. Choosing my words wisely was an absolute must. I knew if I didn't, my feelings would continue to hurt.

Acknowledging my feelings wasn't easy. It required me to pause and be radically clear and honest with myself—not just about my emotions, but about my role in letting the imbalance persist. Acknowledgment didn't mean pointing fingers or blaming my friend, which I had to make peace with. Instead, it meant sitting with the discomfort of what was true and accepting that I was the one who felt hurt and disappointed.

So with that, I had to be the one to ask myself some hard questions:

Why hadn't I spoken up sooner?

Why was I willing to overextend myself without voicing my needs?

Was I holding on to this friendship out of love, or was it more about obligation and fear of losing

someone I cared about and had known for a long time?

Naming the resentment allowed me to release some of its hold on me. For so long, I had been operating from a space of confusion, sensing unspoken tension in our connection but not understanding what it was or why it lingered. Once I could pinpoint the root of the issue, I could move toward clarity. This acknowledgment didn't fix anything overnight, but it was a crucial first step in finding a resolution. It created space for intentional action—room to decide how I wanted to show up in the relationship moving forward and what boundaries I needed to set to protect my heart, peace, and connection with her. I valued our friendship and wanted to work through this with her, not without her.

I remember sitting down with my journal one evening, writing out everything I had been feeling, brain dump style: no edits or self-censoring, just raw honesty and emotion. I started with the resentment, how exhausting it felt to be the only one initiating communication, how unsupported I felt, and how that lack of reciprocity weighed on me. I let myself lean in fully, even though it felt whiny and annoying. But as I kept writing, I began to explore my own accountability. My resentment wasn't solely about my friendship. It was about me and my patterns.

What had stopped me from speaking up earlier?

What fears or assumptions had I been holding on to?

Was I afraid my friend would dismiss my feelings?

Was I scared that asking for more would result in rejection or even losing the relationship altogether?

The more I wrote, the more I realized that I had made assumptions about my friend's intentions. I convinced myself that Eva's lack of effort meant she didn't care about our bond, but I hadn't actually given her the opportunity, clarity, or communication to show up differently. Being quiet or reserved about what was bothering me became a form of self-protection, but it also created distance and prevented the relationship from growing. This reflection gave me the courage to have an honest conversation with Eva. When I finally shared my feelings, I led with vulnerability instead of fault. I explained that I valued our friendship deeply but felt disconnected because I often took the lead in maintaining our friendship. To my surprise, Eva wasn't defensive. In fact, she was grateful I had spoken up.

Compassionately, she shared that she hadn't realized I was feeling this way and admitted that she'd been in her own world. She also shared that I've always taken the lead, and because of that, she put me in that role, and I didn't seem to mind.

That conversation was a turning point. I needed that honesty from her. We both heard each other in new ways when we had this conversation. Being honest and clear with each other allowed us to rebuild our connection with greater intention and mutual understanding. Eva began initiating plans more often, and I, in turn, gave myself permission to pull back when I needed rest—communicating clearly with her when I needed space. The resentment I had been carrying began to dissolve, replaced by a renewed sense of balance and reciprocity.

Sometimes acceptance means moving on without closure.

This experience taught me an important lesson about the power of acknowledgment. It's not about fixing everything immediately or demanding instantaneous change from others. It's about creating transparency—first within yourself and then within the relationship. When you name what's true, you give yourself the gift of choice. You can decide what action to take, what boundaries to set, and how you want to move forward.

In dealing with this, I was also reminded of the importance of communication. Check-ins and touchpoints in our friendships are necessary in more ways than one. Relationships thrive on honest dialogue. Sometimes we must take the first step, even when it feels vulnerable. By naming what we feel and sharing that with those closest to us, we create space for repair, respect, and reconnection in more authentic and aligned ways. Acknowledgment is a practice, not a one-time event. It needs ongoing self-reflection and a willingness to be honest, even when the truth is uncomfortable. But it's through this practice that we create room for openness, healing, and growth.

Here's what I've been exploring in my journal and my daily life years after this experience with Eva. You might find these practices useful, too.

Acknowledge

Acknowledgment begins with seeing what is true. It's a

vulnerable act of honesty with yourself and others, a necessary first step to moving forward. You cannot address what you refuse to name. Lately, I've been asking myself hard but clarifying questions about my relationships:

- Is this relationship nourishing me, or is it leaving me depleted?

- Am I showing up out of obligation or authenticity?

- Are we meeting each other or missing each other?

Taking a few moments each day to reflect on where your energy is flowing is sacred. Jotting down what feels balanced and what feels strained can give us good information and discernment. By naming our feelings and needs, we create space for clarity rather than letting our thoughts swirl in uncertainty. When I realized that I was carrying some resentment in my friendship with Eva, acknowledging it didn't mean blaming her—it meant being honest with myself about how I felt. That simple acknowledgment allowed me to move from confusion to clarity, creating room for intentional action.

Accept

Something that continues to be a teacher in my life is welcoming the idea that acceptance is not resignation. It's an act of grace. This continues to shape and change my heart for the better, especially in the face of adversity. To accept is to release the tension of unmet expectations and say, *"That is where they are, this is where I am, and that is okay,"* even if it's not what you hoped for. One lesson that's been both painful and liberating is this: **People prioritize what they value, and their priorities won't always align with yours.** Instead of trying to force alignment, I've been practicing patience with myself and others. For example, I initially felt hurt when someone I was becoming friends with—let's call her Maya—stopped checking in as frequently. Maya and I weren't close, but we did like each other a lot. When we did connect, we could pick up the phone and talk for hours, sharing everything from our big dreams to the mundane details of our day. Our newly budding friendship felt easy and low-lift from the start. One day, the calls and texts started dwindling. I couldn't help but feel a sting of rejection, but I told myself not to personalize it. Everything isn't about me or something I did. Maybe she's busy, I told myself. Or maybe she's just tired—or perhaps it's family stuff since that had always been a pain point for her. But as the weeks turned into months, I couldn't ignore the growing space between us. It felt personal, even though I didn't want to admit it. I started questioning everything: Had I done something wrong? Was she upset with me? Did she not want to be friends anymore? The silence felt like a void, and I was filling it with assumptions that were not helpful.

One evening, after another unanswered text, I reached for my journal to make sense of the emotions swirling inside me. Writing has always been my refuge, the place where I untangle the knots in my mind, and that night, I let it all spill onto the page—the sadness, the confusion, and the disappointment I hadn't fully acknowledged until then. As the words flowed, a moment of clarity emerged, almost like a whisper cutting through the noise:

> *I can only do what I can do. I know I didn't do or say anything wrong. Our last conversation was warm and kind. Whatever she's going through, it's not about me.*

That simple truth felt like a lifeline, pulling me back to center. I realized how much energy I had spent spiraling into a narrative built on assumptions and fear—wondering if I'd somehow caused this distance or if I wasn't enough in the relationship. But in that moment, I could see how much of the story I had written in my head was just that—a story. None of it was rooted in fact, only in my insecurities around abandonment. Naming this truth softened something inside me. It reminded me that relationships are not immune to life's ebbs and flows, that sometimes people step back not because something was done wrong but because of something they're going through. I also had to be clear about what type of people I wanted in my life for the long run—coming to terms with the fact that Maya and I may not share the same sentiment around building and deepening friendships. It wasn't easy to let go of the idea that I could correct or contain the situation, but accepting that it wasn't mine to fix brought me a sense of relief and a much-needed exhale.

Acceptance in this situation reminded me of something crucial: Her distance wasn't about my worth. It was about where she was on her journey. That realization didn't erase my disappointment, but it softened it. It allowed me to hold space for both my feelings and hers without needing to assign blame or make it a reflection of my value or her character. I decided to reach out again to Maya, but instead of asking when we'd catch up or why I hadn't heard from her, I sent a simple message:

Hey, I just wanted to check in and see how you're doing.
I know life has been a lot lately, and I want you to know
I'm here for you if you need anything.

Maya replied the next day. She told me how overwhelmed she'd been and didn't want to bring me into her drama for fear of feeling like a burden. She admitted that she'd withdrawn not because she didn't care but because she didn't know how to ask for the space she needed without feeling like she was letting me down. She said:

> You're such a good person. You're present, kind, and thoughtful. I want to be your friend, but I cannot reciprocate right now. I do not have the space.
> I'm sorry.

I cannot explain how happy I was to read those words. Her honesty was exactly what I needed. Accepting Maya's truth made a lot of things make sense. I replied:

> Maya, I hear you and understand completely. Take good care of yourself. I hope you know how worthy you are of care, kindness, and support. Should you ever need a friend in me in the future, I am willing to pick up where we left off.

> Thank you, Alex. I appreciate that more than you know.

We never spoke again after that, but I had clarity, making acceptance easier to move through. This experience reminded me of the power of grace for ourselves and others. Accepting where Maya was, allowed me to approach the situation with compassion instead of judgment. It also taught me a valuable lesson about relationships: Sometimes, people need distance to heal, grow, or simply survive. Their pulling away isn't always a rejection; it's often a reflection of their own capacity in the moment. Now, when I think back on that season of our friendship, I don't see it as a time of loss. I see it as a time of learning. I learned to let go and to trust. I recognized that acceptance isn't about settling for less; it's about meeting people where they are and deciding how to move forward from there. I know that true friendship has room for ebb and flow—it's not about always being perfectly aligned, but about holding space for each other, even when things get messy or the timing isn't right.

Maya and I didn't find our way back to each other's lives, but even if we had, the heart of the lesson remains the same: Sometimes acceptance isn't about mending a relationship or bringing it back to what it once was. It's about making peace within yourself—letting go of what you cannot control and finding closure, even without closure. In that stillness, I found gratitude—not for the distance, but for the clarity it brought. Acceptance asks: *Can you hold what is true without trying to make it something else?* It invites you to stay grounded in your worth, even when the circumstances around you shift.

Adjust

Adjustment is where freedom lives. To adjust is to honor your needs and boundaries without resentment. It's deciding to meet people where they are—or choosing not to meet them at all. Think about one relationship that feels out of balance. Maybe you're always the one prompting connection, or perhaps you've been holding space for someone who never seems to have the capacity to hold space for you. Adjusting doesn't mean cutting people off, but it can mean recalibrating your effort to reflect your truth. Pouring from an empty cup is not sustainable. Constantly doing the most and feeling unsupported in return is a crappy feeling to have in rotation. Adjusting, for me, meant stepping back—not as punishment, but as a self-care practice.

For example, a fellow author and I collaborated on a project, but it quickly became clear they expected me to shoulder most of the work. Eventually, I decided to stop being the one who constantly checked in, offered support, and followed up on their tasks. Instead, I let them take the lead to show how they wanted to contribute. Their communication became inconsistent, and a few opportunities fell through. While it wasn't the outcome I had hoped for, it was a valuable reminder that I couldn't take full responsibility for their part of the work. By stepping back, I was able to protect my energy and refocus on my own priorities. Adjustment reminds us: You are not selfish for wanting relationships that feel reciprocal and safe. You are simply honoring the love you deserve.

By putting the three A's into practice—acknowledge, accept, adjust—you reclaim your power. You begin to find clarity, not just about what you want, but about what truly is. This clarity helps you make peace with the gap between what you hoped for and what reality offers. It's not about giving up or settling; it's about seeing things clearly and letting go of the struggle to force them into something they're not. By doing so, you create room for gratitude, even in the hardest moments. You learn to release what no longer serves and embrace what aligns with your growth. If there's one thing I hope you take away, it's this: Peace is found in the present, not in chasing what could be. You are worthy of connections and experiences that bring balance to your mind, body, and spirit—and sometimes that balance starts with accepting things as they are.

Reflections

- In what ways have you been honest with yourself about the needs and dynamics in your friendships and relationships? Are there any patterns or behaviors you've been avoiding or overlooking?

- How can you cultivate compassion and understanding for yourself and others as you navigate the imperfections in your relationships? What truths about these connections are you ready to embrace or change without resistance?

- What shifts can you make to better align your friendships and relationships with your values and needs? How can you approach these changes with care and clarity?

- Reflecting on acknowledging, accepting, and adjusting, where have you experienced growth in how you communicate your boundaries and expectations in relationships? Where have you gone along to get along?

- When conflict or misalignment arises, how can you use the three A's to respond rather than react, fostering deeper understanding and connection?

The right people will not only listen—they will hear you with their whole hearts. They will make space for your feelings, honor your needs, and remind you through their actions that you are valued, cherished, and seen.

PART

TWO

TWELVE

CHOOSING CLARITY OVER COMFORT

HAVING HEALTHY AND SUPPORTIVE RELATIONSHIPS WITH people, especially our friends, is not only possible but invaluable. However, cultivating these relationships requires honesty, clarity, and a willingness to speak up—especially when silence feels safer. Unspoken silence does not create a connection; it can shatter it. Why? Because shutting down doesn't foster closeness, it creates roadblocks that are difficult to navigate. When we retreat into ourselves, withholding our truth to avoid discomfort, we make room for resentment to take hold rather than creating an opportunity for a vulnerable connection. The challenge is to push through the instinct to withdraw and instead lean into what strengthens bonds: communication, accountability, and emotional reciprocity.

In my early twenties, I had a close friend named Jennifer. Our friendship had always felt solid, but this interaction showed me how easily distance can grow without communication and transparency. One weekend, I excitedly texted Jennifer to see if she wanted to go to a local art exhibit we had both been talking about. We planned to check it out together, so I assumed she'd be excited, too. She responded with a short, *"Can't."* That was it. No explanation, no follow-up. I felt a little off about her reply, hurt even. My bubble of excitement had been burst instantly. And instead of asking if everything was okay and if we could find a day that worked for us both, I got in my feelings and withdrew. At twenty-one, I used silence as my go-to feeling-sparer. Of course, that wasn't healthy in hindsight. However, we do what we know until we learn differently. We've all been there at some point. Then, of course, I started to overthink and create a story in my head about how I'm always the one putting forth effort and that I was *done* doing that. With no words spoken, I let the ball be in her court. I told myself that if she wanted to check in or reschedule, she would.

Days turned into weeks and the space between us grew. She said nothing, and neither did I. Without clarity or context, I told myself that if she wasn't reaching out, I wouldn't either. My emotional immaturity was showing big time. Six weeks passed before we finally reconnected, and I learned that on the day I reached out, she had been dealing with a difficult family situation and wasn't in a place to make plans.

Immediately, I felt like a jerk for assuming instead of asking. My first question to her was, "Why didn't you tell me? We're friends, sisters damn near. I don't understand."

"I didn't want to dump all of that on you," she admitted. "I figured you had enough going on, and I didn't want to be a burden."

That stopped me. I had never once thought of her as a burden. I would have shown up without hesitation if she had told me she needed support. But instead, she had chosen silence, and I had mistaken that silence for a lack of interest in our friendship.

"Is that why I haven't heard from you? You were angry with me?" Jennifer asked.

In shame, I hung my head and said, "Yes, I was upset. But I'm sorry—I should've asked you what was going on instead of making it about me."

"I'm sorry, too—I could've used my words, I guess," she said with a smile to lighten the mood.

At that moment, we vowed to be clear with each other from there on out. We've kept our word and are still close friends all these years later. That experience made me realize how often we assume we are protecting each other by holding things in when, in reality, distance only creates more confusion and more distance. It also helped me recognize how my own reaction played a role. Instead of leaning into curiosity and asking, *"Hey, is everything okay?"* I had chosen to be overly sensitive, internalizing her short response as rejection rather than pursuing clarity. Getting quiet on each other didn't serve our friendship or create leeway for mutual consideration. Whether we are twenty-one or sixty-one, over-personalizing situations without gathering context creates unnecessary tension, whereas direct communication can help us foster trust.

Our conversation—or lack of it—was proof that it is easy to misinterpret silence. I assumed Jennifer's response was about me, but it wasn't. I had let an unspoken expectation create distance instead of inviting clear communication into the equation. Friendships need compassionate directness, not quiet speculation. Instead of waiting for someone to notice our silence, we need to be willing to communicate.

Below are some examples of how this could've been handled better in case you find yourself in a similar situation.

||||||||||||||||||||||||||||||||||||||||||||

How Jennifer Could Have Handled It Better

Instead of the short, vague response of *"Can't,"* Jennifer could have provided more context, even without going into detail. Something like:

"Hey, I'm dealing with something today and need to lay low, but I still want to go! Can we find another day?"

This response would have acknowledged my invitation while also setting a boundary. It would have reassured me that she wasn't shutting me out, just that she needed space in that moment. A simple acknowledgment can go a long way in preventing misinterpretation.

How I Could Have Asked for Clarity Instead of Shutting Down

Rather than assuming her short response meant she didn't value our friendship, I could have checked in with a simple, direct message:

"No worries! Everything okay?"

This would have allowed her to share—if she wanted—while showing care without pressure. If I was feeling disappointed, I could have expressed that in a non-accusatory way:

"Got it! I was looking forward to going together, but I totally understand if today isn't a good time. Let me know if you want to plan for another day!"

Approaching it this way would have communicated my feelings and given her a chance to clarify rather than leaving space for assumptions. No one technically "owes us" an explanation, but context is a beautiful gift when we are in relationships with others. In healthy friendships, clear communication helps build trust and harmony. On my end, rather than assuming the worst and pulling away, I could have chosen curiosity over jumping to conclusions.

It's important to remember something deeper: Letting the people in our lives know that their struggles are not "too much" for us is beautiful. Jennifer had been struggling alone, but instead of sharing, she held it in out of fear that I had enough on my plate. How often do we do this to the people who care about us—decide for them what they can or cannot handle? In trying to protect them, we can unintentionally push them away. This instance in our friendship also reinforced how over-personalizing situations does not support healthy relationships or honest communication. Taking everything as a personal slight instead of considering different perspectives creates unnecessary conflict. Clarity is key—not just for ourselves, but for the people we care about. Friendships thrive when we approach moments of uncertainty with openness. The relationships we're in and nurturing do not require constant availability or contact, but they benefit from small moments of clarity. A few extra words can prevent days—or even weeks—of unnecessary distance and untrue stories. By choosing communication over withdrawal, we intentionally create friendships where honesty, vulnerability, and transparency are the foundation, and misunderstandings don't have the chance to take root.

The first step in strengthening our friendships is looking inward. Everything isn't about what someone else is or isn't doing. Sometimes, it's about us. How do we show up in our friendships? Are we clear about our needs, or do we expect people to intuitively understand them? Do we communicate our boundaries or silently hope they'll be respected without conversation?

I used to pride myself on being the friend who always understood, never needed anything, and could be counted on without question. I thought this made me a good friend. It took years—and plenty of heartache—to realize that what I had called loyalty was often self-erasure. I stayed in friendships where my needs were secondary, where my silence made space for others but left no room for myself. And when those friendships faltered, I blamed myself, wondering what more I could have done. The truth was, I needed to learn that friendship isn't about over-functioning. It's about reciprocity. The conversation with Jennifer allowed me to acknowledge this out loud and change my thinking and behavior moving forward. I had to start understanding that Jennifer wasn't like my old friends or family members who expected me to be seen and not heard.

Holding myself accountable and being emotionally mature enough to use my words created a new sense of safety within my relationships. I learned that my silence wasn't self-protection—it was self-abandonment birthed from fear of being rejected. Choosing clarity over comfort invites more depth and trust into our friendships.

When We Get It Wrong

Accountability in friendship isn't just about recognizing when others have let us down but also acknowledging when we've fallen short. We will get it wrong sometimes. We will miss a moment when a friend needed us. We will say something careless, withdraw when we should have leaned in, or let our anxieties dictate how we respond to their needs. None of this makes us bad friends; it makes us human.

Over the years, I've seen that what defines a strong friendship isn't perfection but the ability to repair when conflict arises. Jennifer and I have been friends for a decade and some change, and we have gotten really good at being clear. When we come to each other in a tender or challenging moment and say, "Hey, this hurt me," without hesitation, we now recognize that a call-in is an act of care, not an attack. Collectively, we must remember that it takes courage to express pain and trust to create a moment of connection from that hurt. If we ignore the people we call friends in a moment of conflict or let silence fester, we uproot closeness and can, in turn, slowly dismantle the friendship.

To this day, Jennifer and I continue to work on choosing to listen, even if we disagree or don't understand. Pausing to reflect on what the other is saying rather than reacting out of our own discomfort creates a sturdy ground for sift-

173

Gentle Reminder: Friendship is a choice.

ing through issues, qualms, and misunderstandings. It's an act of love to say and show, *"I hear you. I see how that impacted you. That wasn't my intention, but I take responsibility for your feelings. What can I do to make this right?"* Jennifer and I used all those questions when we hit a growing pain in our friendship. This, to me, is how we handle each other with care and consideration.

Friendship is a choice. Love is a choice. And both require action over passivity if we want them to grow the roots necessary for true connection. We cannot expect deep, nourishing friendships if we are unwilling to engage in the work of emotional honesty. Friendship won't always flow effortlessly, and the reality is that even the most soul-aligned friendships require hard conversations and care. Years later, I was reminded of this truth when one of my clients, Marissa, came to me in tears over an increasingly one-sided friendship. The moment she started describing her situation, I had a flashback to my experience with Jennifer all those years ago—the assumptions, the silence, the quiet resentment that created more distance than necessary.

Marissa told me that she was always the one who reached out first. She was the one who adjusted her schedule. She was the one who listened and supported without hesitation. But her friend was absent, distracted, or too busy when she needed the same.

"I don't want to be needy," Marissa admitted. *"But I need people, too."*

That sentence struck me deeply because, in a way, Jennifer and I had both played roles in this dynamic before—me, assuming that if she cared, she'd reach out; Jennifer, thinking that if she shared her struggles, she'd be burdening me. Both of us had let silence widen the gap rather than choosing clarity. Through our work together, Marissa realized that her core fear in friendship was being perceived as too much or too sensitive, which kept her from expressing her needs. She had convinced herself that a good friend absorbs, accommodates, and never asks for anything. When she finally spoke up, her friend's reaction was telling—defensive, dismissive, unwilling to engage. It was painful, but it was also clarifying. Marissa had spent years giving to someone unwilling to meet her halfway. And with that clarity, she chose to step back, making room for friendships where she could be valued rather than just useful. Listening to her story, I felt even more grateful for learning how to communicate and listen in my own life and relationships. Jennifer and I had also been at a cross-roads, but we leaned into the hard conversations instead of letting discomfort drive us apart. We chose to ask instead of assume, to express instead of withdraw. And because of that, our friendship didn't just survive—it deepened.

On the other hand, Marissa's situation revealed something different: Sometimes, when we choose clarity, we also gain the courage to walk away from friendships that no longer nourish us.

Whether it's a friend like Jennifer who holds back out of fear of being a burden, or a dynamic like Marissa's where one person does all the emotional labor, silence does not foster connection—it fractures it. Both situations reveal why over-personalizing things or assuming the worst doesn't serve anyone. If I had chosen curiosity with Jennifer instead of shutting down, we could have avoided unnecessary distance. If Marissa's friend had valued reci-procity, their friendship might have had a chance to grow instead of remaining one-sided.

So, the next time you feel yourself withdrawing or assuming the worst, pause. Ask. Express. Because clarity is not just an act of self-care—it's an act of care for the peo-ple we choose to call friends.

DEEP DIVE: Reflections

1. **Reflect on a Recent Friendship Challenge.**
   - Did you express your true feelings or hold them in?
   - How might honesty have shifted the outcome?
   - What did you need in that moment, and how might you approach a similar situation differently in the future?

2. **Accountability in Friendship.**
   - Recall a time when a friend called you out or held you accountable for something you said or did.
   - How did you respond—were you open to their feedback, or did defensiveness take over?
   - Looking back, how could you have responded in a way that honored both your perspective and the friendship?

3. **Recognizing Patterns in Friendship.**
   - What patterns do you notice in how you give and receive support in your friendships?
   - Are there relationships where you feel drained or unseen?
   - Are there friendships where you feel safe, valued, and deeply understood?

4. **Defining Your Friendship Needs.**
   - Write down three qualities you need in a friendship and three that you offer in return.
   - How does this clarity help you strengthen your current friendships or make peace with releasing the ones that no longer serve you?

5. **The Power of Honesty in Relationships.**
   - When was the last time you avoided an uncomfortable conversation in a friendship?
   - What was the cost of avoidance—did it create distance, resentment, or misunderstanding?
   - How can choosing honesty over comfort help you cultivate deeper, more nourishing friendships?

6. **Letting Friendships Evolve.**
   - Consider a friendship that has changed over time.
   - How have your needs, priorities, or values shifted?
   - What would it look like to embrace this change with honesty and grace rather than holding on to an outdated version of the connection?

7. **Being Seen and Understood.**
   - Think of a friend who truly sees and

understands you. What makes that friendship feel safe?

- How can you be more intentional about showing up in the same way for others?
- In what ways do you want to be more open and seen in your friendships?

8. **Friendship and Boundaries.**
   - Have you ever said "yes" in a friendship when you really wanted to say "no"? What led to that decision?
   - How can you practice honoring your own boundaries while still being present and caring?
   - What would it look like to create relationships that respect both your needs and your friend's?

9. **Clarity as a Compass.**
   - What friendships feel like a natural extension of who you are?
   - What relationships require you to shrink, overextend, or abandon parts of yourself?
   - What shifts—small or big—can you make to ensure your friendships reflect your truth?

10. **Friendships That Sustain You.**
    - Who in your life makes you feel deeply understood and valued, even in your imperfections?

- How can you nurture and pour into those relationships with more presence and care?
- How does it feel to know you are worthy of friendships that nourish and sustain you?

Being clear is
an act of love.

THIRTEEN
RADICAL RESPONSIBILITY

A S MUCH AS WE LONG FOR RECIPROCITY AND BALANCE in our relationships, the real work begins when we turn inward and ask ourselves: *How am I contributing to the dynamics I find myself in?* Personal accountability isn't about self-blame—it's about self-awareness, self-compassion, and bravery in addressing your roles in certain cycles. This reflection is the bridge between personal growth and healthier connections with others.

If self-awareness feels difficult, you're not alone. It's a skill we all have to learn and practice over time. Learning to be accountable for your own thoughts, feelings, and behaviors doesn't show up overnight—it requires patience and intentionality. For years, I found myself frustrated by friendships that felt one-sided or stagnant. I'd focus on what the other person wasn't doing: how they weren't showing up or how distant they seemed. But the truth was, I was so preoccupied with their behavior that I neglected my own. When we fixate on what others are doing—or failing to do—we lose our sense of agency. We start overreacting, overthinking, and letting ourselves drift off course. Shifting the focus inward is uncomfortable and hard, but it's the only way we reclaim our power and find clarity about what we need, what we're willing to give, and where we draw the line.

A client of mine, Shayna, once shared a story about a falling-out she had with her friend Hope. Shayna felt hurt and unappreciated because Hope hadn't reached out in months. This wasn't the first time they had a conflict like this. It was a pattern they'd fallen into—one of them would be going through something difficult and pull away, and instead of reaching out or addressing the distance, the other would do the same. Both of them avoided communication altogether, each waiting for the other to make the first move.

Shayna interpreted Hope's silence as a lack of care. She told herself that if Hope valued their friendship, she would have reached out by now. The story Shayna created in her head fueled her resentment, and as a result, she started to withdraw, too. "I'm so tired of being the one who always checks in, makes plans, and shows up," she told me. And I could understand her frustration—most of us have felt that way at some point. But the truth is, passive aggression and unspoken expectations only widen the gap in our relationships. Learning how to lean in and use our words is vital. Trying to control the narrative by not saying anything isn't helpful because it leaves room for speculation to take the place of truth. Silence can feel safer than vulnerability, but it seldom brings the clarity we need. When we withhold our feelings, we may protect our pride, but we also block the potential for understanding and repair. Real connection requires courage—the kind that allows us to say, *"Hey, I miss you,"* or *"I felt hurt when I didn't hear from you."* It doesn't guarantee the response we want, but it does give the other person a fair chance to show up with honesty and care. Communicating openly isn't about control—it's about creating space for truth, even when uncomfortable.

Eventually, the distance between them grew unbearable—and Shayna decided to stop hoarding her hurt feelings and have an honest conversation with Hope. She shared her frustration, expecting an apology or explanation. But instead, Hope surprised her by saying, *"I didn't know you felt this way. I thought you were upset with me because I hadn't heard from you, either."*

In that moment, Shayna realized how much damage her silence had caused. She had been so focused on her feelings of hurt and rejection that she hadn't considered her role in their unhealthy dynamic. By withdrawing and waiting for Hope to make the first move, she was contributing to the very disconnection she resented. Through our work together, Shayna started to understand how harmful passive aggression and avoidance can be in any relationship.

She began to see that her silence wasn't neutral—it was loud in its own way. It sent a message, even if it wasn't the one she intended. The longer Shayna held back, the more room for resentment grew. The outcome of that made it harder to bridge the growing distance. I had Shayna do some writing work to start peeling back the layers of why using silence as a protector was her go-to. In those deep dives on the page, she realized that her pattern of waiting to be pursued was rooted in an old belief from childhood—don't speak unless spoken to, unless you're wanted around. That inner-child wound walked with her into adulthood, forming the belief that if someone cared, they would prove it by coming to find her. That belief shaped how she navigated closeness. Shayna refused to ask for what she needed. Instead, she waited, hoped, and hurt when her unspoken needs went unmet. Through our writing work together, Shayna began naming these early messages for what they were: survival strategies that had once protected her but now kept her stuck in patterns of emotional idleness and pain.

Together, we worked through prompts like, *What am I expecting others to know without me saying it?* and *What does my silence try to control?* Slowly, she began connecting the dots between her past and present behavior. She wrote about memories where speaking up was met with dismissal or criticism and how, over time, she learned to make herself small to stay safe and easy to handle. But during our coaching sessions together, Shayna started to understand that safety and silence are not the same thing, and it was time to reclaim her voice—not just to use it in relationships, but to hear herself more clearly.

Letting go of our old stories is not low-lift soul work, which is why I believe writing to heal is such a beautiful way to explore self-awareness, accountability, and compassion. With each entry, Shayna grew more willing to challenge the part of her that equated silence with strength. She started to see that resilience is built on self-awareness and choice—not on waiting to be handpicked when it's convenient—and that was the turning point: when she stopped waiting to be invited into connection and began practicing what it meant to just start showing up. Once Shayna could own her part—not with shame, but with curiosity and compassion—she opened the door for healing.

Replacing our assumptions with genuine and truthful conversations helps us to start practicing what it means to lean in rather than shut down.

I often hear a variation of this from my clients: *Silence and unspoken assumptions feel like self-protection.* And while that may feel true in the moment, when we peel back the layers, those two things only lead to more disarray and discomfort. Relationships thrive on honesty, not hidden expectations or unspoken issues. Accountability isn't about blaming yourself—it's about recognizing your part in the dynamic and choosing to show up differently.

When Shayna started communicating her needs openly and addressing patterns with clarity and compassion, her friendship with Hope began to heal. More important, Shayna started to practice showing up for herself— acknowledging her feelings, expressing her needs, and

Shift your focus.
Reclaim your power.

choosing connection over avoidance. Did things always go as planned or how she wanted them to go? Of course not. However, the goal was never perfect outcomes—it was the commitment to honest and clear participation within her interpersonal relationships.

Shayna and Hope knew they wanted to stay friends, but there was a lot of reprogramming to do for the two of them. Sometimes, they were able to respond with openness with each other, and other times, they needed space before leaning in. Regardless of the outcome, the friends felt more grounded because they no longer abandoned themselves to keep the peace or prove a point. Speaking up might feel risky, but staying silent often costs us more in the long run.

Shayna and I worked together for three months, and by the end of our time together, I was so proud to see that she started journaling to unpack the past and prepare for hard conversations—writing out what she wanted to say, what she was afraid of, and what she needed in order to feel supported. This practice became a bridge between intention and action. And over time, those small, consistent acts of self-honoring began to reshape how she related to others. Shayna wasn't just healing her friendship but also mending her relationship with herself.

No relationship, not even one with yourself, can thrive without honest communication.

When Shayna started to take ownership of her role in the dynamic, she also began to embrace small but powerful practices that strengthened her relationships—starting with herself. Here are some practices we did together to help shift her patterns and build healthier bonds with others.

Pause and Reflect Before Reacting

When emotions feel overwhelming, it's easy to immediately act on hurt or assumptions. Learning to pause and ask yourself, *What story am I telling myself right now? Is this based on facts or feelings?* can help us gain clarity before jumping to conclusions or withdrawing.

Practice Honest, Direct Communication

Instead of waiting for people to notice our frustrations, expressing them in real time, without blame or passive aggression, can be helpful. Using "I" statements, like, *"I've been feeling disconnected and hurt, and I want to talk about how we can better show up for each other,"* is one way to create a space for mutual understanding.

Release Expectations of Mind-Reading

One of the most freeing lessons Shayna told me she learned during our coaching was this: *People can't read your mind.*

If you need something—whether it's more frequent check-ins, reassurance, or help during a tough time—speak up. This doesn't make you needy; it makes you clear. Being clear is an act of love.

Set Boundaries Around Resentment

The weeds of resentment can become unruly when unmet needs and expectations go unspoken. It is essential to learn to notice when resentment is creeping in and use it as a signal to check in with yourself. Ask yourself, *Is there something I need to express or a boundary I need to set?* Paying attention to the start of resentment before it takes root and evolves is a powerful tool for self-awareness.

Take Responsibility for Your Role

Accountability isn't self-blame—it's empowerment. A part of the homework I gave Shayna was to regularly ask herself, *How am I contributing to this dynamic?* This question helped her stop focusing solely on what others weren't doing and start making changes within herself that aligned with her values.

Engage in Relationship Check-Ins

Shayna and Hope started scheduling regular check-ins to talk about how they were feeling and what they needed in their friendship. These intentional conversations helped them avoid falling into old patterns of distance and miscommunication.

Show Up for Yourself First

Perhaps the most transformative practice for Shayna was learning to prioritize her emotional health first and foremost. She journaled about her feelings, checked in with her therapist, worked through her assumptions on the page with me, and gave herself the grace to grow through it all. By showing up for herself, she was better equipped to show up intentionally versus being overwhelmed by others.

As Shayna discovered, healthy relationships aren't about perfection but intention, transparency, and mutual effort. Start by looking inward if you're stuck in a cycle of silence or assumptions. Ask yourself what you need, communicate it compassionately, and remember that relationships are built one honest conversation at a time.

Things to Remember

Accountability isn't about self-blame; it's about self-awareness. It asks you to pause and reflect:

- Am I communicating my needs? Or expecting others to read my mind?

- Am I holding space for others the way I want them to hold space for me?

- Am I showing up consistently? Or withdrawing out of fear, frustration, or assumption?

- Am I contributing to the balance of this relationship? Or am I silently building resentment?

The lesson here is simple but profound: **You cannot expect what you are unwilling to give.** If you want honesty, bring honesty. If you want grace, extend grace. If you want connection, lean into vulnerability. Effort begets effort. Accountability also teaches us to be more open by reminding us that relationships are co-created. When we take ownership of our actions and reactions, we create an atmosphere where others feel safer doing the same. It shifts the dynamic from blame to curiosity—from *Why didn't they?* to *What am I bringing into this?*

Accountability invites a kind of emotional humility that softens defensiveness and builds trust. It doesn't mean tolerating mistreatment or over-functioning to keep the peace; it means staying rooted in our truth without abandoning our values. It teaches us that we can hold others accountable while still holding compassion. And when we live that balance, we model a more honest, spacious, and emotionally responsible way to connect. The truth is, we're all human. Sometimes, we fumble through connections, trying to get it right while sometimes getting it wrong.

A Practice of Accountability

Accountability isn't about judgment—it's about expansion. It allows us to see where we've fallen short and to celebrate where we are showing up with care and intention.

Here are a few reflection questions to explore on your own.

- Did I show up with integrity and authenticity?

- Did I take the time to truly listen to the people I love?

- Did I hold space for their experiences without letting my assumptions get in the way?

- Where can I do better next time?

Shayna and Hope's situation shows us that personal accountability is freeing, but it has to be a deliberate practice met with reciprocal effort. It can give us all the power to create change. It reminds us that while we cannot control how others show up, we have autonomy in how *we* do. When we approach accountability with empathy and curiosity, we have the power to bolster our relationships and deepen our connection with ourselves.

FOURTEEN

FINDING YOUR PEOPLE WITHOUT CHASING THOSE WHO FLEE

T HERE'S A HARD TRUTH MANY OF US AVOID BECAUSE IT scratches at our hope: The people who are running from us are not our people. No matter how softly we speak, how much we accommodate, or how earnestly we try to connect—if someone is emotionally unavailable, uninterested, or consistently inconsistent, it's not our job to perform for their attention or chase after their affection. Relationships, in any form, are meant to be a two-way street. They thrive not when one person tries to build a connection while the other pulls away, but when there's mutual presence, effort, and consideration. One thing I've learned the hard way more times than I can count is that the people meant for you won't require you to shrink, explain your worth, or have you pleading to be chosen. They'll meet you in the middle and show you they're just as certain about you as you are about them.

Now, I know relationships aren't black and white. Sometimes, our connections feel like they're in a gray area. However, being realistic and honest with ourselves and the company we keep brings the truth back into focus—and the truth isn't always easy to accept or swallow.

I used to believe that love meant endurance and that if I just kept showing up for people—always being available, silencing my true feelings, not rocking the boat, and repeatedly giving chances—they would eventually meet me halfway. But I learned, each and every time, that performing effort with the hopes of staying in someone's life isn't authentic. Trying to control our relationships by pretending to be someone we're not is guaranteed to hit the fan in the worst way. People-pleasing might buy us temporary harmony, but it can't sustain authentic connections. Eventually, grievance will creep in—either because we become exhausted from suppressing our true selves, or because the people around us sense something is awry. Real friendship thrives on honesty and mutual vulnerability, not performance. When you give yourself permission to show up authentically, you create space for bonds built on acceptance rather than approval.

*y*ears ago, I watched someone I loved deeply—full of joy, conviction, and warmth—shrink inside a slowly unraveling relationship. They were the kind of person who lit up when they talked about building a life with someone. My friend desired monogamy, stability, and creating a life with someone who chose them, fully and entirely. But the person they were with didn't share those sentiments.

Their partner kept things vague—open to everything, committed to nothing. When my friend asked for clarity, they were often met with slippery words dressed as reassurance: *"You know I care about you. Why do we need to complicate things? Isn't my telling you I love you enough?"* But it wasn't enough—not for someone who was longing to be loved in actions, not just in theory. I watched as my friend began to contort themselves in small, painful ways. They stopped bringing up their needs out of fear of "being too much." They laughed off things that hurt. They convinced themselves that love meant being endlessly flexible and endlessly understanding. And month after month, I saw the light in their eyes dim. Their certainty about self-worth began to erode, replaced by quiet self-doubt and a growing ache they couldn't name.

What was once a vibrant, grounded soul slowly morphed into someone I barely recognized. I watched my friend change in the short time they were in this relationship. Witnessing them walking on eggshells, apologizing for wanting to be chosen, and settling for less was tough. And still, they stayed because hope can be a powerful tether, especially when it's tied to the version of someone we *wish* existed. I knew those feelings well.

Watching that relationship unfold up close taught me a lesson I won't forget: When we shrink ourselves to fit inside someone else's uncertainty, we set the stage for self-

Release performing. Stand in authenticity.

abandonment. I watched my friend pour so much energy into someone who never fully showed up. It was like watching them reach for a door that stayed just barely open—just enough to keep hope alive but never wide enough to walk through. Their partner kept them on an emotional roller coaster—affectionate one day, distant the next—offering just enough to keep them hooked but never enough to feel secure. There's a particular kind of heartbreak in watching someone you care about slowly disappear under the weight of a relationship that only ever gives in fragments.

My friend poured so much into proving they were worthy of staying. It was heartbreaking. Witnessing the over-extending, over-explaining, over-functioning—hoping that if they just showed up perfectly, loved harder, and asked for what they wanted, they'd finally be chosen. Saying it was painful to witness would be an understatement. And no matter how much effort they gave, it never made a difference. The truth is you can't out-love someone's avoidance. You can't earn consistency from people who thrive in the muddled middle. And you cannot anchor yourself to someone who refuses to stand with you. I wanted to shake my friend and say, *"You don't have to prove anything. You are already enough. You deserve a love that runs toward you, not away."* But as many of us know, when you're in it—when your heart is all tangled up in potential—it's hard to see the difference between someone choosing you and someone showing you they don't want you in the way that you want them.

For a long time, I tried to hold space. I wanted to stay close and remind my friend who they were when they forgot—but eventually, I had to completely remove myself. Why? Because witnessing someone you love abandon themselves repeatedly in real time is a slow kind of heartbreak. I was grieving the version of them that used to speak with clarity, that used to know their worth, that used to stand tall in their truth. No matter how gently I tried to reflect back their power and be a mirror of their worth, they couldn't see it through the fog of their relationship.

I began to realize that my presence was starting to feel like pressure. Even though it came from a place of love, my concern was being felt as criticism. And the last thing I wanted was to become another voice my friend felt they had to defend themselves against. So I stepped back—not out of anger, but out of care. Sometimes, the most loving thing you can do is stop trying to rescue someone who is telling you they don't want or need to be saved. There will be moments when space is the only mirror clear enough for someone to truly see themselves. And even though it hurt, I knew that continuing to hold on and trying to be a steady support—while they were deep in the middle of figuring out their life and relationship—wasn't helping either of us grow or heal. At times, coming back home to ourselves can only happen in solitude. And in the end, even our most painful pursuits lead us back to the same question we can't escape: *What would it feel like to stop chasing someone and start choosing myself instead?*

Things to Explore

Being a Mutual Mirror

When someone you love is disappearing inside a relationship—shrinking, settling, or self-abandoning—it can be hard to know when to stay close and when to lovingly step back. While you're reflecting on your own relationship or holding space for someone else, think about these things:

- Am I (or are they) being chosen in action, not just in words?

- Is there room for my/their full self here— or just the parts that are easy to love?

- Am I (or are they) constantly overcompensating to keep the connection alive?

- Is my presence bringing clarity, or is it starting to feel like pressure?

If the answers point toward imbalance, it may be time to create space—for you, for them, or for the truth to rise without interference.

Flexibility Isn't Self-Betrayal

There's a difference between being flexible and being forgotten—even by yourself. I watched my friend try to convince themselves that their willingness to bend was love. That compromising their values, swallowing their needs, and tolerating inconsistency was a form of emotional maturity. My friend consistently said they were being understanding. Patient. Supportive. But I, and others close to them, saw someone slowly disappearing to keep in proximity to a person who had no intention of meeting them where they were.

That's the danger of unchecked flexibility. It starts as compassion, but it can quickly turn into self-erasure. We think we're being loving by adjusting, but sometimes what we're really doing is shape-shifting to be tolerable to someone who hasn't made room for us to be whole.

Real flexibility is rooted in mutual respect. It's a two-way street. It says, *I see you, and I'm willing to grow with you*—not *You stay still while I contort.* When flexibility costs you your voice, needs, or truth—it's not love. It's self-betrayal dressed up as loyalty.

The Disappearing Act Check-In

Use this check-in when you find yourself (or someone you love) constantly adapting in a relationship. Flexibility should feel like spaciousness, not self-abandonment. Ask yourself:

- Am I softening my needs? Or silencing them completely?

- Is this compromise being met with reciprocity—or just convenience?

- Do I still recognize myself in this relationship? Or have I started performing a version of me that's easier to love?

- Am I adjusting because there's shared growth here? Or because they've made it clear they'll leave if I stay true to who I am?

If your answers reflect fear, exhaustion, or deep disconnection from yourself, it's a sign that your flexibility may be crossing into self-erasure. Healthy love and friendship don't require you to disappear. On the contrary, your connections should allow you to bring your full self to the table—and be met there with care.

Letting Go of Attachment Doesn't Mean Letting Go of Love

Stepping back was never about giving up on them. It was about releasing the illusion that I could love them into clarity. That if I held on tightly enough, they'd finally see what I saw—their worth, their beauty, the weight of what they were giving away just to feel wanted.

But love without boundaries quickly becomes a burden. And concern, even when rooted in care, can sound like criticism when someone is already questioning their choices. I didn't want to be another reason they felt the need to defend decisions they weren't fully at peace with. I tried to remain a soft place to land—not another pressure point in an already tender season.

So I let go. Not out of anger, but love. I had to release the urge to fix, convince, and save. I chose quiet compassion over constant intervention. I chose trust—trust that they would find their way, even if the path were longer or more painful than it needed to be. Letting go of attachment doesn't mean you stop caring. It means you trust in someone's ability to return to themselves, even if the journey looks nothing like you hoped. After all, it's not *your* journey. At times, detachment means offering your presence without an agenda. Your love without conditions or expectation of an outcome. And your heart without demanding anyone sees things the way you would, or think they should. Because real friendship—real love—knows when to lean in, and when to lovingly release.

The Curiosity Practice

When someone you care about is in a relationship that's draining them—or when you're the one starting to lose sight of yourself—it can be tempting to react with urgency, frustration, or advice masked as love. But curiosity offers something deeper than control: it invites clarity without force.

Instead of pushing or fixing, try opening the door to gentle, reflective dialogue—whether with yourself or someone you love:

- "What part of you is holding on to this connection?"

- "Who are you becoming in this relationship— and do you like that version of you?"

- "What do you need more of in this season— support, space, or self-trust?"

- "What would it feel like to stop proving your worth and simply come home to it?"

This kind of curiosity doesn't demand change—it makes space for it. It doesn't rush someone's process—it honors it. When we lead with questions instead of judgment, we remind ourselves and those we love that growth isn't something we force—it's something we remember.

Because sometimes, the most powerful thing we can offer isn't an answer. It's a safe, judgment-free space for someone to ask their own questions—and hear what rises to the surface.

Let What's One-Sided Fall Away

At some point, we have to stop calling it a connection when we're the only one doing the holding. The only one reaching. The only one showing up with consistency, care, and truth. One-sided relationships don't just break our hearts—they confuse our sense of self. They teach us to settle for breadcrumbs while convincing ourselves it's a feast. And in the process, we begin to question if we're asking for too much when, in reality, we're just asking for the basics: reciprocity, respect, and commitment. It's difficult to let go of anyone you once imagined building with, romantically or platonically. It's painful to walk away from the potential, the history, the hope. But we can't keep trying to plant roots in places that only offer temporary shelter. Choosing to release a one-sided relationship isn't bitter. It's bold. It's saying that *I'm no longer available for connections that require me to abandon myself to stay connected to you.* It's choosing mutual effort over continued longing, presence over promises, reality over potential. When we stop chasing, we don't lose love—we make space for the kind that stands firmly, stays present, and meets us in reciprocity. Fully. Freely. Without having to shrink to fit.

Letting go might hurt, but staying in something lopsided has proven that it can slowly drain your spirit. As I told my friend (and myself) multiple times: *You deserve to be met with the same depth, care, and commitment you offer.*

The Self-Return Check-In

STEP 1: TAKE INVENTORY WITHOUT JUDGMENT

Over the course of a week, gently notice the energy exchange in the relationship.

- Who initiates?
- Who listens and follows up?
- Who makes time, not just excuses?
- Write down what you observe. Let patterns reveal themselves without needing to force a conclusion.

STEP 2: ASK YOURSELF HARD— BUT HONEST—QUESTIONS

- Am I the only one keeping this connection alive?
- Do I feel safe, supported, and seen here—or just tolerated?
- Have I been silencing myself to keep the peace?
- What would change if I stopped chasing and started choosing myself?

- Let your answers speak plainly. You don't need to explain them away. You just need to listen.

STEP 3: RECLAIM YOUR BELONGING

If your answers reveal a lack of reciprocity, it may be time to let go—not in anger, but in alignment. Create a quiet, intentional moment to mark your return to yourself.

- Write a release letter to the relationship. Say what you need to say without censoring yourself. You don't have to send it—this is for you.
- Light a candle, go for a walk, or sit in stillness and say aloud: I no longer abandon myself to feel close to someone else. Moving forward, I will choose to honor my worth.
- List three core values you want to lead with in future connections—mutuality, consistency, emotional safety, or whatever feels most true to you.

STEP 4: PRACTICE DAILY SELF-HONORING

Commit to one small, nourishing practice each day that reminds you who you are and what you deserve—whether that's journaling, meditation, movement, or simply saying no when you mean it.

SAYING GOODBYE WITH GRACE

FRIENDSHIP, AT ITS BEST, IS A SACRED MIRROR—ONE that reflects not only who we are but who we're becoming. When B and I first connected, it felt like one of those rare, serendipitous alignments. The kind that reminds you it's still safe to hope for new beginnings. At the time, it was what I needed. And I know it was what she needed, too.

Our friendship gave us something beautiful—a glimpse into what it feels like to be met with reciprocity, to not have to explain why intentional communication matters, and to be chosen consistently and with care. We built something honest, rooted in emotional safety and shared values. That chapter in my life—our chapter—taught me how nourishing it is to be in relationships that feel easeful, mutual, and spiritually aligned.

But even sacred things can shift.

Over time, something between us began to change. It wasn't dramatic or sudden. Just a slow, quiet unraveling. I noticed myself questioning how to show up, unsure if my presence would be received with the same warmth. That kind of doubt doesn't come out of nowhere—it arrives when energy shifts and clarity fades into confusion. I knew what it was, but out of respect and care for B's and my bond, I won't be sharing the intimate details on these pages. Nevertheless, eventually, I reached a crossroads. Holding on quietly felt heavier than letting go lovingly.

I chose clarity over cowering and sent a message from the heart:

Hey, hi. I'm really glad you had a beautiful day before your vacation and that therapy is giving you what you need. You deserve it! Wishing you safe and fulfilling travels.

I've been sitting with our conversation from a few weeks ago, and as much as I appreciate the honesty we shared, the shift between us is loud. Our friendship is different, and truthfully, it doesn't feel like we'll find our way back to the closeness we once had. That feels sad and it also feels true.

There's a hesitation now—a distance. I've come to accept that our place in each other's lives has changed. And that's okay. I expected this after what came to light. I think both of us wanted the friendship to return to "normal," but truthfully, things feel awkward now. The ease and lightness feel far away, and I find myself second-guessing even reaching out at all, in fear of being too much or a bother—which doesn't sit right with me.

I could be wrong, but maybe our friendship arrived when we needed it most, showing us what sisterhood could look like—and that was the purpose of our closeness before January 1, 2025. I'm deeply grateful for meeting you and sharing in friendship with you. It was truly healing. I don't want our connection to slowly fade or feel unclear. I think that would be even more hurtful/ confusing. I do not know what the future holds, but for now, I think it's best we go our separate ways. You are such a special person, and I'm thankful for our friendship. It pains me to send this message, but I hope you know how glad I am that we got to know each other.

I truly wish you the very best this life has to offer. I hope you have peace in all the places that matter most in your world.

Sending love, always.

—A.

Her response was full of grace, I wasn't expecting anything different from her:

Hi. Thank you for being honest with me—it means a lot. I want you to know that I hear you, and I truly respect the courage it takes to speak your truth. Gaining insight into how things have felt from your side helps me better understand the shift between us.

To be honest, your message caught me off guard. While I was aware that our rhythm had changed, I hadn't sensed the same distance you've been feeling—especially after our last conversation. It makes me realize that we may need different things from sisterhood, and that's okay. I respect your decision to part ways.

I never want anyone close to me to feel uncomfortable or unsure in our connection. That kind of dissonance stands in the way of real closeness, and it's not something I want the people I care about to carry.

I'm incredibly thankful for everything we've shared—our laughter, our long walks, the vulnerable moments, and all the in-betweens. I've said it before, but it's still true: you're one of the most creative, inspiring people I've had the privilege to walk beside. Take good care. Keep shining. I'll be cheering you on from afar.

—B.

Reading her message, I felt a deep exhale. No bitterness. No blame. Just truth, clarity, and love. Letting go doesn't erase the good. It simply honors the fact that not everything is meant to last forever. Some people walk with us through a specific season. When that season ends, it's not a failure. It's a sacred completion. This ending reminded me of how much I've grown. I no longer avoid hard conversations or take shifts in connection personally. I trust what fades. I trust what flows. I trust myself to move when something no longer aligns.

After her message, I sent one final reply:

Thank you for this compassionate reply. I appreciate it a lot. My needs and desires around sisterhood and friendship haven't changed. For clarity, it's not about the cadence for me. I don't need or want to constantly communicate with anyone in my life. It's about the energy—it's not the same. And given all that happened

in January—of course there's been a shift. That's human.
We were both jolted and that's hard to come back from
sometimes.

Regardless, given the things you shared at the top
of the year and a few weeks ago, I absolutely respect
where you are. I also don't ever want how I show up,
show love, or anything else in between to create a
feeling of overwhelm, intimidation, etc. From what
you've said multiple times in different ways, it sounds
like that occurred. You said to me multiple times
that you felt unworthy of this friendship. You know I
wholeheartedly do not agree, but I also deeply believe
that our friendships and relationships shouldn't cause
us anxiety. I know you have a lot on your plate to
sort through, and there are no hard feelings from me
that our capacity to hold this friendship like we once
did has changed. I'm so proud of us for being able to
speak openly and honestly. I hope ease, clarity, and joy
continue to find you in this life. I will always be rooting
for you, too.

—A.

In that moment, I felt a deep sense of self-trust. The
version of me who used to shrink to keep the peace no lon-

ger exists. I lead with my full self—kindly, clearly, and un-apologetically. I know now that the right people will meet me in that truth.

Hours later, I got a message from B that said:

You've been truly heard. I want to take a moment to acknowledge the bravery it took to express yourself so openly with me—thank you for that. This morning, I allowed myself to sit with the grief and sadness that came up, and eventually, I found myself arriving at a deep sense of peace and reverence.

There's something calming about knowing that while things have changed, the space between us feels steady. I'm in awe of how we've allowed this relationship to evolve naturally, with mutual respect and grace. I'm proud of how we've navigated this shift together.

Thank you for helping create a sense of closure that feels honoring to both of us. I'm holding you in love and hoping for harmony ahead for us both.

It's no surprise that two strong, creative Leo women found such a meaningful connection. This chapter was beautiful. I'll carry the joy, lessons, and love forward with me. You are deeply appreciated.

Learn when to lean in and trust when to let go.

This experience taught me that you can love someone and still need to walk away. You can honor the good while acknowledging when the connection no longer fits. You can release something with grace and still hold it with deep, unwavering gratitude. I've worked hard to become this woman. One who is devoted to emotional honesty, compassion, and care even in the sticky or tender moments. The older I get, the more I realize that I don't long for "friends" that fill voids and lack depth. I crave friendship. The kind that is active, accountable, and rooted in mutual care, even if that means parting ways for now or for life. I carry the lessons of friendship and relationships as a whole, with love into every space I enter. Whether teaching, mentoring, or in everyday connection, I remind myself and others that truth-telling is not abandonment but devotion. It is care. It is sacred clarity.

Relationships that require us to guess, perform, or

shrink are not fertile ground for connection. I hope, after reading this book, we all feel a little more grounded and capable of building a life rooted in aligned love, mutual energy, and conversations that leave no room for confusion.

Letting go of my friendship with B was a human, humbling, and clarifying experience. It reminded me of what I value and am unwilling to compromise on. I think it showed her similar lessons. It taught me that closure can be kind—that endings can be clean. And that the love we share and offer to others is never wasted. If anything, it's multiplied. Some friendships are forever. Others are for a moment that leaves a lasting imprint. This one was both.

Accepting the shifts in our relationships—especially ones that once felt like home—is one of the hardest things we're called to do. But a part of emotional maturity is learning how to release with love instead of clinging out of fear. We often resist letting go because we're attached to the version of the relationship that once brought us comfort. However, when a friendship begins to slip, we feel it. We sense the hesitation in the responses, the energy that once flowed freely now needing to be explained, managed, or chased. No matter how much we may want to return to what was, sometimes the kindest thing we can do—for ourselves and others—is to let it be what it was and not try to force it to be more. There are times to lean in and times to let go.

When something starts slipping away, we can either

grip tighter or soften our hands. I've learned that holding on too tightly can turn a once beautiful bond into something burdensome. That doesn't mean we didn't love well. It could mean, though, that we're learning to love more wisely, and maybe even differently. All relationships require work, but work doesn't need to be consistently hard. Unfurling our grasp can lead to more liberation. It doesn't always mean giving up. To me, it can represent observing the truth of the moment—choosing to live in alignment with what is, not what we wish things still were. The space that opens up after release is often the exact space we need to grow. Sometimes what we think is the end is actually a new beginning—the beginning of choosing ourselves, our peace, and our relationships that pour back into us with clarity and care.

Each of us deserves to be in friendships where the connection feels clear. Where we don't have to over-explain our needs or minimize our presence to maintain stability. When a relationship starts feeling like it's barely holding on, and talking about things isn't creating a change, it may be time to set it down gently. Not with resentment—but with reverence for what it taught you and appreciation for the chapter it offered. We are all a work in progress. None of us are exempt from the messiness of learning, unlearning, and trying again.

Being deliberate in our friendships—choosing to show up with clarity, care, and courage—is an emotional muscle that requires practice. It's not something we master overnight, or maybe ever. But it takes honesty, repair, and a willingness to keep tending to the relationships that matter with intentionality. Some days, we get it right. On other days, we miss the mark. But when we stay committed to evolving in how we love and allow ourselves to be loved, we create relationships that are not only resilient but deeply rewarding. Over time, we begin to understand that the company we keep is a reflection of how well we honor our values, our boundaries, and our hearts.

Guiding Questions for the Road Ahead

- What does it mean to you to be truly met in a relationship—not tolerated, not managed, but deeply understood?
- Whose presence in your life has taught you the difference between being needed and being valued?
- What silent agreements have you outgrown— agreements that once kept the peace but now cost you your truth?
- When you think about relational safety, what does it look, sound, and feel like in practice— not theory?
- Have you ever mistaken intensity for intimacy? What do you now know about the difference between the two?
- Who have you felt most emotionally generous with, and did that generosity feel mutual—or one-sided?
- What unspoken rules have shaped how you show up in friendship or family—and which ones are ready to be rewritten?
- What role does repair play in your

relationships? How do you know when someone is capable of doing the work of healing with you?

- What does it feel like in your body when you're in a room where you can exhale fully? Who helps you feel that way?
- How do you want to be remembered by the people you love—and what kind of company are you keeping that supports that legacy?

ACKNOWLEDGMENTS

THIS BOOK WOULD NOT EXIST WITHOUT THE MANY RE-
lationships that shaped me, stretched me, and softened me. I am grateful for the love that held me, the
tension that taught me, and the moments of rupture that
led me back to myself.

To Ryan—thank you for being my foundation and
naming this book. To my daughters—thank you for teaching me what it means to love with intention and show up
with truth. You are my greatest teachers.

To my friends, past and present—your presence, honesty, and evolution helped me discover what sacred con-

nection truly looks like. Whether you stayed for a season or remain for a lifetime, your impact is felt.

To my readers and community—you make this work matter. Thank you for showing up again and again with open hearts and curious minds. You remind me that we don't have to navigate life alone and that healing is richer when we do it together.

To my agent—thank you for carrying me gently throughout my career and holding me accountable. Your support stretches me. I am endlessly grateful for your bond, personally and professionally.

To my editor, Anna, and the entire team at Tarcher— thank you for your belief in my vision and for bringing it to life with care and enthusiasm. I am grateful.

To everyone who is learning to choose themselves without guilt, to trust their intuition, and to keep company that honors their wholeness—this book is for you.

With deep gratitude,
Alex

Alexandra Elle IS A WRITER AND RESTORATIVE WRITing teacher. In her work, Alex aims to build community and healing practices through language. She is the author of several books and journals, including, most recently, *How We Heal* and *After the Rain*. She has been featured by prominent media outlets such as the *New York Times*, NPR, *Good Morning America*, ABC News, *Essence*, The Cut, MindBodyGreen, BET, and *Forbes*, among others. Alex teaches workshops, courses, and retreats to assist others in finding their voices and creating clarity in their lives and relationships. She lives in Maryland with her family.